Praise for *Why I Believe*

"Chip Ingram has a way of taking complex and intimidating material and making it accessible and applicable to everyone."

Kyle Idleman, pastor, author of *Grace Is Greater*

"We all need straight answers to the questions we ask about God, faith, and the Bible. Chip Ingram helps us to get our hearts and minds around the most important issues we face and offers authentic and transparent answers."

Jack Graham, pastor of Prestonwood Baptist Church, Plano, TX

Praise for *The Real God*

"Chip Ingram provides wonderful insight to help you see God's character as presented in Scripture. In these pages, he offers practical biblical help to live out the implications of a refreshed and renewed perspective of God. The principles in this book will inspire, encourage, and empower you to become more like Jesus Christ."

Rick Warren, founding pastor, Saddleback Church

Praise for *Good to Great in God's Eyes*

"The principles that my good friend Chip Ingram outlines in this book will inspire, encourage, and enable any sincere reader to maximize their God-given potential for the glory of

God and for the good of others. Only read this if you want your life to matter."

Tony Evans, PhD, senior pastor, Oak Cliff
Bible Fellowship

Praise for *Culture Shock*

"Is it possible to articulate timeless biblical truth without resorting to anger and argument? Is it possible to lovingly embrace those with whom we disagree without compromising our beliefs? The answer to both of these questions is a resounding YES—and Chip Ingram explains how it's all possible in this timely and relevant book."

Jim Daly, president, Focus on the Family

DISCOVER
YOUR
True
SELF

DISCOVER YOUR
S *True* LF

How to Silence the Lies of
Your Past and Actually Experience
WHO GOD SAYS YOU ARE

CHIP INGRAM

BakerBooks

a division of Baker Publishing Group
Grand Rapids, Michigan

© 2020 by Chip Ingram

Published by Baker Books
a division of Baker Publishing Group
PO Box 6287, Grand Rapids, MI 49516-6287
www.bakerbooks.com

Printed in the United States of America

Library of Congress Cataloging-in-Publication Data
Names: Ingram, Chip, 1954– author.
Title: Discover your true self : how to silence the lies of your past and actually
    experience who God says you are / Chip Ingram.
Description: Grand Rapids, Michigan : Baker Books, a division of Baker Publishing
    Group, 2020. | Includes bibliographical references.
Identifiers: LCCN 2019041861 | ISBN 9780801093814 (cloth)
Subjects: LCSH: Identity (Psychology)—Religious aspects—Christianity. | Self-
    esteem—Religious aspects—Christianity. | Bible. Ephesians, I–III—Criticism,
    interpretation, etc.
Classification: LCC BV4509.5 .I4375 2020 | DDC 248.4—dc23
LC record available at https://lccn.loc.gov/2019041861

ISBN 978-0-8010-9323-4 (ITPE)

20 21 22 23 24 25 26   7 6 5 4 3 2

I dedicate this book to

Bill, A. C., and Dick,

three mentors and father figures
who helped me discover the real me.
These men believed in who God made me to be
long before I could see it or believe it myself.
Their love, encouragement, support,
and sometimes painfully honest feedback
have shaped my life. I am eternally grateful.

Contents

Acknowledgments

This book has been developing in my heart and mind for many years. Like most followers of Christ, I grappled with what it really means to be "in Christ" and live *from* my worth in Him rather than seeking to gain it through success, productivity, or self-improvement.

Dr. Bill Lawrence, Professor Howard Hendricks, and too many wise teachers to name taught me the theology of my position in Christ, as my wife, Theresa, modeled for me the practical means of replacing lies about myself with the truth of my new standing before God.

Venture Christian Church's elders, staff, and congregation helped me develop and refine the concepts in this book as I first taught them in a series of expositional messages on Ephesians 1–3.

Jerry McCauley's insight, feedback, editing, and oversight of this project were invaluable, and this book would not exist without him.

Chris Tiegreen's wordsmithing and editing of the actual manuscript were foundational as we transformed messages into paragraphs and chapters.

My assistant for many years, Charlotte Coulter, diligently protected my time, managed my schedule, and provided logistical support with tons of encouragement when deadlines and life seemed to collide.

I'm especially grateful to Brian Vos, Mark Rice, and the entire team at Baker Books for their feedback, suggestions, and tremendous flexibility.

Finally, thank you, Theresa, not only for hours and hours of listening to this book but for years of helping me learn to see myself as God sees me. You're the best!

Introduction

The Power of Mirrors

I will never forget an experience I had my senior year in college. After my college basketball team lost a tournament game that ended our season, most of my teammates determined the best way to celebrate would be to go out and party.

By this time, I was walking with the Lord and had no desire to hit all the bars in Charleston, West Virginia, to watch my buddies get drunk. A cheerleader named Mary was of the same mind. She was a friend I knew from a couple of the Bible studies on campus.

After the game, Mary and I found ourselves in a small all-night coffee shop. To be honest, I was more than a little intimidated. She was stunningly beautiful and athletic, with long blonde hair, piercing blue eyes, and a 3.7 grade-point average. Though I had come to believe that no one "had it all together," she seemed to be the exception. She had been blessed to be in that 1 percent of the gene pool.

After listening to her story for about two hours, I couldn't believe what I was hearing. The distance between how she viewed herself and objective reality was stunning.

I'm not exaggerating when I say she seemed to hate herself. She actually looked in the mirror and thought she was ugly and worthless. I tried to encourage her, but when I reminded her of her great GPA, she said, "4.0 is a success in my family. I'm a failure."

I was sitting with someone who had so much going for her in every respect, yet she saw herself as a failure, ugly, and unacceptable.

Her perception was completely illogical to me.

Despite her beauty and her gifts, Mary had multiple mirrors throughout her childhood that told her she was ugly, didn't measure up, and was unlovable. Those mirrors shaped her thinking about herself and, as a result, how she interacted with others.

But after thirty-plus years of pastoring and counseling, I'll tell you this: Mary is not an exception.

The Power of Mirrors

Let me ask you a question: What do *you* see when you look in the mirror?

We look at ourselves in the mirror multiple times a day. There's the mirror in the bathroom that says the makeup looks good, the hair is in place, and that shirt matches the sweater. There are mirrors at the gym that tell us we're making progress—or that we've got a long way to go.

But it's not just physical mirrors that are powerful. We each have mirrors within us:

The mirror of a little boy looking up and catching his mom's first reaction of disappointment.

The mirror of going to middle school, thinking, *Wow, I really look cool in this new outfit,* and then realizing three minutes later in the hallway that you not only don't look cool but people are laughing at you.

The mirror of disapproval from a spouse.

The mirror of a boss who says, "You don't measure up."

The mirror of a coach or teacher who said you were dumb or lazy.

The mirror of the media that says if you don't have a perfect body, you're not acceptable.

These mirrors create a composite picture in our minds and tell us who we are.

Warped Mirrors

I am no longer surprised by how radically people's views of themselves differ from objective reality. The truth of the matter is, we all have warped mirrors.

We all experience distortions, mirrors past and present, that affect our lives and our relationships. It's a lot like when you were a little kid and you went to one of those fun houses where you would walk in front of one mirror and look eight feet wide and then run to the next mirror and look two feet tall and then the next mirror made you look skinny as a toothpick. As children, we laugh when we see ourselves in the distorted images in the fun house mirrors. But there's nothing funny about the distorted mirrors we believe.

When it comes to distorted mirrors, the most powerful influence in our lives is our parents and family of origin: our mom, dad, siblings, or lack thereof.

The second most powerful influence is authority figures, role models, and peers. People we look up to, whose opinions matter—sports heroes, artists, musicians, pop culture icons, and the friends we hang with—all constitute a myriad of mirrors that constantly shape our perception of who we are.

These influences can help us see our gifts, talents, and strengths and positively inspire us. None of our parents were perfect, but many of our best qualities and positive pictures of ourselves flow from them or from a teacher, coach, or role model.

Unfortunately, the same influences can be the source of warped mirrors resulting in:

- Feelings of insecurity, inferiority, or superiority
- A performance orientation (my value is only in what I can do)
- Withdrawal (avoiding risk at all costs as it brings rejection)

- Denial (refusing to look honestly within as it's too painful)
- Compensation (overachieving to prove everyone wrong)
- Addictive behavior (medicating the pain)
- Unfulfilled longings for significance and acceptance

While there are multiple self-help resources and tools to address all kinds of dysfunctions, the root cause of many of our problems is an inaccurate view of ourselves.

What we need is a mirror that is trustworthy, a mirror that allows us to see ourselves as God does.

Where Can We Get an Accurate View of Ourselves?

I have good news for you: *There is a mirror that never lies.* It's objective and accurate, and it will tell you who you are, how much you matter, and why you're here on earth.

That's what I want for you.

I want to help you break free from deep-rooted misbeliefs, relational patterns that never seem to change, and internal struggles that seem to have no solutions. The mirror I'll show you is a divine one, given to you by God to help you see yourself as He sees you.

Despite what you've heard, despite what's been planted in your conscious and subconscious mind about who you are, what you're worth, and what others think of you, God declares that in Christ you are wanted, valuable, secure, competent, beautiful, and called for a purpose only you can fulfill.

In the chapters that follow, I identify the lies that have held many of us prisoner for years. We will look at the pain and the struggles they have caused us and learn specific and practical ways to replace those lies with the truth.

Theologian A. W. Tozer observed that "what comes into our minds when we think about God is the most important thing about us."[1]

Here's the second most important thing about us: *what comes into our mind when we think about ourselves.*

Will you join me on a journey to shatter the distorted images and lies we believe about ourselves?

PART 1

WANTED

1

The Lie of Rejection

For years, Billy watched couples come into the orphanage in search of a child to adopt. For years, he watched his friends get chosen. Billy was still there at the age of eight—past the stage of cute, past the typical age of adoption.

Left out and *rejected* became part of his identity.

Eventually, a husband and wife did come and adopt Billy. For the first time in his life, Billy had a bedroom of his own, enough food to eat, and a family who loved him. Yet his new parents found him sleeping on his floor. "What are you doing?" they said. "We have a bed for you."

Billy didn't feel worthy to sleep in a bed.

On another occasion, Billy's parents discovered food in his closet. He had snuck it out of the refrigerator and hoarded it in his closet because that's what he had always done. In the orphanage, he was never sure if he was going to get enough to eat.

While there, Billy had fended for himself—never feeling loved, never feeling worthy, never knowing what it meant to be accepted. In reality, he had been legally adopted by a father and mother who loved him. He'd been given a new name and provided a caring home.

But that wasn't enough to undo years of rejection.

For years after he was adopted, Billy kept his orphan identity. When he grew up, God called him into the ministry. He was bright and a hard worker, and he became a successful church planter and pastor. However, Billy still felt that sense of rejection, so he went to school to get degree after degree, running after whatever he felt would make him acceptable.

The Second Most Important Thing about You

Unfortunately, there are a lot of people like Billy who are loved and accepted but still live with an orphan identity.

It took a long time for Billy to overcome his identity as rejected and unwanted, but by God's grace, he did. Billy was William D. Lawrence, the Dallas Theological Seminary professor who taught me to preach. In fact, it was his mentoring and counseling that helped me see myself the way God does.

Let me ask you a couple of very important questions about your identity. First, *what is your image of God?*

A. W. Tozer taught us that "we tend by a secret law of the soul to move toward our mental image of God."[1] He also said that "what comes into our minds when we think about God is the most important thing about us."[2] It is essential for us to get a high, holy, clear, accurate picture of who God really is, because our perception of God has such a powerful effect on our lives. A distorted image of Him will take us pretty far off track in life.

Now, if you agree that it's vital to have an accurate picture of who God really is to understand your identity, then another question is equally important: *How do you see yourself?*

> *One of God's primary desires is for us to know who we really are in His eyes.*

Because I believe that the second most important thing about you is how you see yourself.

If we are going to see God accurately, we need to know something about His perspectives, including His perspective of us—what He thinks about when He looks at us. One of God's primary desires is for us to know who we really are in His eyes.

We need to learn what He had in mind when He created us, and what He wants and expects from us in our relationship with Him. God longs for us to see ourselves the way He sees us.

How Do You See Yourself?

In your mind's eye, how do you picture yourself? What do you believe about who you really are?

Knowing everything you know about your appearance, your thoughts and feelings, your deepest needs and biggest dreams, your skills and talents and flaws, how would you describe yourself honestly?

Are you loving and caring? Warm and approachable? Gifted, smart, and innovative? Powerful and persuasive? Lonely, inadequate, and insecure? Confused or fearful? Feeling lost or purposeless? Angry and resentful? Too tall, too short, too thin, too fat, too . . . anything?

For now, don't describe the person you want to be. How do you actually see yourself?

This perception is what psychologists call your self-image. It's the mental image you have of your own identity and self-worth. In other words, it's a composite of all the mirrors you look into in order to see who you are.

Your New Identity

Many of our self-perceptions go much too deep to be wiped away with some corrective self-talk. But we can identify the lies we believe and renew our minds with God's truth. In doing so, we will significantly change the course of our lives.

No matter how painful your memories and emotions are when you think of your past, you can experience healing and restoration. That's what redemption is all about. Whether you perceive yourself positively or negatively, getting a vision of *your true self* through God's eyes is transforming.

It was for my wife Theresa and me. It changed the entire direction of our lives. It even saved our marriage. When I began to see myself as a wanted, valued, and deeply loved *son* of my heavenly Father, I no longer demanded Theresa to make my life work and meet all my needs.

Scripture tells us to think about ourselves accurately—not too high, not too low, not *too* anything. In Romans 12, the apostle Paul commands us to have an accurate perception of ourselves:

> For by the grace given me I say to every one of you: Do not think of yourself more highly than you ought, but rather think of yourself with sober judgment, in accordance with the faith God has distributed to each of you. (v. 3)

Notice that this instruction is given in the form of a command. It is not just friendly encouragement, a pat on the back, or a helpful suggestion. It is not presented as an option. We are told not to think of ourselves inaccurately but in accordance with sober judgment and with the faith God has given us—in other words, the way He sees us.

When we trusted Him as our Savior, we died with Him, our sins were forgiven, and we were justified in His sight, meaning we were declared legally righteous. All our sins— past, present, and future—are now forgiven. The moment we placed our faith in Christ, the righteousness of Jesus Himself was given to us, and God sees us now through the lens of His Son. We are reborn in the Son's image; this is our new legal standing before our heavenly Father, whether we are living up to that image or not.

Through the lens of the sacrifice of Jesus and His cleansing blood, God sees us as clean, righteous, forgiven—as His children.

The really big implication of this amazing truth is that God loves us as much as He loves Jesus.

Let me ask you a question: What does it mean to be *in Christ*?

If we are in Christ—in other words, if we have a real relationship with Him, not based on church membership or some standard of moral behavior but on genuine faith in Him—we are made new.

> *God loves us as much as He loves Jesus.*

We are *in Him*, and He is *in us*, and God sees us as He sees Jesus. These are not merely theological concepts or religious words. This is the new and eternal reality of everyone who has trusted in Christ and His work on the cross for the forgiveness of their sins and entrance into God's family.

We tend to emphasize justification and the born-again experience—entering into salvation by grace through faith. And that's huge, so it ought to be emphasized. But tragically, many Christians spend their lives focusing on what we are saved *from* without ever realizing what we are saved *for*. A real and profound journey begins with salvation, and it involves living as a son or daughter of God who *no longer has anything to prove*.

When we enter into a relationship with our heavenly Father, we have a new standing. He gives it to us. We don't have to try to earn it anymore. We don't have to try to become a son or daughter or demonstrate that we belong in the family. We already have His favor.

Our elder brother, Jesus, is at the right hand of the Father, and He wants us to live out of the love we have been given. Learning how to do that may be a journey, but becoming who we are is not.

He has already given us a completely new identity: *We are sons and daughters of the Creator.* However, getting that reality from our heads to our hearts is no easy task.

The Lie: Rejection

My wife, Theresa, never heard her father say, "I love you," and she can't remember getting hugs from him. But she does remember the pain of feeling rejected.

Like many girls who don't get the love they need from their father, Theresa looked for it in unhealthy ways. To escape her home life, she was married young to someone who confirmed her sense of unworthiness. Human nature often draws us to whatever feels normal rather than what is right and good. After she put her husband through college, he began selling drugs and cheating on her. Then, when she gave birth to twins, he left her for the other woman.

Theresa experienced the pain of rejection all over again. But thanks to the witness of her boss, she came to know Jesus. She accepted the truth that God loved her and wanted to have a personal relationship with her. I met Theresa when the boys were two and a half years old, and we became friends. Her life had been transformed. Her overwhelming sense of need had caused her to lean into God's love like few people I'd ever met.

About a year later we started dating, and eventually, we got married. But eighteen months into our marriage, I wondered if it was going to work. I realized that even though my wife loved Jesus and had accepted the truth of the gospel, she still had a deep sense of unworthiness. She was beautiful, smart, loving, talented, and passionate about God, but when she looked in the mirror, she saw someone who was a reject, someone unworthy of being accepted. She literally couldn't believe or receive my love.

Sitting in a counselor's office trying to sort out the roots of our problems was painful. By God's grace, our counselor realized that beneath all the psychological issues and my wife's warped view of herself was a bigger problem: She needed to see herself the way God saw her. She needed to stop believing the lies about her own self-worth.

Our counselor told Theresa to write down the misbeliefs she held on a card—for example, MISBELIEF: "I need other people's approval to be happy." Then, at the bottom of the card, she would draw a stop sign followed by "TRUTH: I want people's approval, but I don't need it. With God's approval, I am no longer compelled to earn love and acceptance. I am free to be me." The counselor would provide a Scripture passage that expressed that truth—in this case, about belonging—and Theresa would read it over and over again.

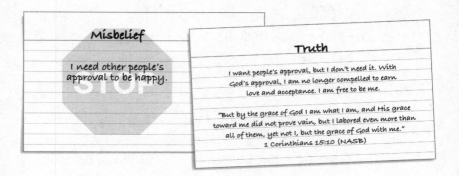

Misbelief

I need other people's approval to be happy.

Truth

I want people's approval, but I don't need it. With God's approval, I am no longer compelled to earn love and acceptance. I am free to be me.

"But by the grace of God I am what I am, and His grace toward me did not prove vain, but I labored even more than all of them, yet not I, but the grace of God with me."
1 Corinthians 15:10 (NASB)

For two years, we went over those cards together every morning before I went to work because our marriage depended on it. A lot of ugly, dysfunctional patterns had developed when we had a warped view of ourselves.

People who feel rejected may become people pleasers at all costs. Many become overly sensitive to criticism because it comes across as another form of rejection. And many withdraw to avoid any possibility of rejection, preempting the rejection they assume will come by removing themselves from relationships before it can happen. Avoiders are reluctant to take risks or to engage in certain activities where they might get hurt. People pleasers can be enormously successful because they get up earlier and work harder in order to achieve more. Behind some of the world's greatest achievements are deeply insecure people who fear rejection—scared people who believe their value is based solely on what they do and how they appear. All of these responses have a way of distorting, undermining, and potentially destroying our relationships.

Before we go on, let me ask you: Which of those unhealthy responses do you most closely identify with? Go ahead, be honest. We all have them, and as you'll learn, being honest is the first step to lasting change.

You Are Wanted

As I helped my wife review those cards and work through her deep issues, I realized I had all the same issues. I struggled with rejection just as much as she did, but I masked it better. In fact, I had learned to use it to my advantage. My fear of rejection was driving me to perform, to achieve, and to succeed. I was being rewarded for my workaholic dysfunction.

But only to a point. I was so focused on overachieving and being successful that I ended up in the hospital being treated for exhaustion—twice. A doctor told me my immune system was depleted and asked what I was doing to myself. I told him my schedule, and he told me I was "on an unhealthy and destructive path to burnout."

My point is that all of us believe lies about ourselves. And we need to come to grips with those lies and replace them with truth.

We need to see ourselves as God sees us. As long as we hold distorted views about ourselves, we will be driven by unhealthy motives, strive for unnecessary validation, and develop dysfunctional relationships. Worst of all, we will not be able to experience the fullness of the gospel of grace, because we will always be searching desperately for something more.

Only when we realize that God views us as deeply loved children will we begin to live in freedom and experience fulfillment.

So, let me ask you again: How do you really see yourself?

Let's face it, we all have distorted pictures of our identity that undermine our relationships and rob us of contentment. If you're like me, I'm guessing you can relate to struggles with rejection.

Why? Because none of us has a perfect self-image or a complete understanding of who we are in Christ. We all wrestle with insecurity at some level, whether we are aware of it or not. We all have that experience of trying to be a "somebody," even though God has already made us to be incredibly valuable and loved. We still live like orphans in spite of having been adopted by a loving Father.

This journey of discovering your true self begins with identifying what you think about yourself, measuring your perception against what God thinks of you, and learning how you can narrow the gap between your view and His.

God longs for you to see yourself as He sees you: *wanted*.

Questions for Reflection and Discussion

1) What are some of the mirrors that influence your identity?

2) Fear of rejection is universal. Can you relate to Billy and Theresa? What about their stories resonates with you?

3) The trials and traumas of human relationships can distort the way people view themselves. What life experiences have affected your perception of yourself?

4) In Romans 12:3 NASB, we read that we have been given a "measure of faith" with which we can learn who we are in Christ. According to this picture of the truth, how should you think of yourself?

5) What distortions about your identity have you embraced to the point of seeing them as reality, even if your mind tells you they are not true? List them and identify them as lies. Pray and ask God for His help in seeing yourself the way He does.

2

You Are Wanted

Ephesians 1:1–6

Craig didn't have a lot of friends in high school. In fact, he really didn't have any at all; most of his "friends" were only acquaintances, and he felt lonely most of the time. Like most teenagers—like everyone, actually—he was desperate to belong to something: a team, a club, a clique, anything. He lived with a constant sense of rejection.

Through some acquaintances at his church, Craig was eventually drawn into his youth group and began to feel a sense of belonging. The group seemed safe. *People at church have to accept me, even if the rest of the world doesn't*, he thought. *They're supposed to love everybody.*

And as naïve as that thought may have been, it held true in this case, at least with most of his peers. Craig was made to feel accepted, even if he never quite fit in with the most popular kids. Being on the margins of a group was better than being in no group at all. Craig semi-belonged.

One of the best ways to belong in any group is to notice what that group values, promotes, or celebrates and then to position yourself at the center of those things. In a church, what's most valued is very often the selfless ministers and missionaries who make great sacrifices. Over time, Craig began to sense a call to ministry, partly from true and pure motives, and probably to some degree to feel more accepted in those circles.

Just as he had felt drawn to the church by his need to belong, he felt drawn to ministry in order to belong even more, to be one of the insiders. So, he pursued a career in ministry, but more specifically, in missions. That was what his church celebrated most, a person who gave his life to serve Christ on the mission field. Whether he actually had the skills for that kind of career was beside the point. His heart, his sense of calling, and his life values all pointed toward missionary service.

Craig spent a few years in pastoral ministry, and then he moved to Asia under an appointment by a missions organization. He loved the cross-cultural experience, learned the language, and spent most of his time thinking about all the ways the gospel should and could be expressed in culturally appropriate forms—yet he generally failed in his ministry efforts.

He became a great example of living life on two levels. On one hand, he was driven with a true sense of calling and real theological understanding of what life is all about. But on the other hand, he was driven simultaneously by a deep need to be someone important, to be loved and admired and respected.

He didn't know who he was. His theology had inspired his life, but it hadn't healed his heart.

Where We Get an Accurate View of Ourselves

Craig desperately wanted an identity that God had already given to him through salvation. But because he hadn't grasped that identity, his view of himself was distorted.

That's almost always the way it is with the driving forces of our lives. They are mixed. It's entirely possible to have true, Spirit-inspired motives to belong, serve, and bear fruit for the sake of Jesus and His kingdom on one level, while also having a desperate need to belong, serve, and bear fruit for the sake of being accepted as a *somebody*. The healthy and the unhealthy drives are often intertwined—two distinct but converging streams running alongside each other in a person's heart.

One of the best pictures of our identity is found in Paul's letter to the Ephesians. Ephesus was a huge metropolitan city, one of the largest in the Roman Empire and a regional hub in Asia Minor. Any letter written to the church there would be read and circulated among several other churches. For this reason, it's not surprising that Ephesians addresses a number of issues that are foundational to our relationship with God and our identity in Christ. The first half of the letter deals with what we have received and who we are in Christ; the second half addresses the implications—how we live in light of the gospel relationship and identity we have received.

Taken as a whole, Ephesians presents a powerful picture of what it means to be redeemed, enlightened, empowered, and equipped to live as new creations in a universe in which God has already defeated all the powers of darkness. It is a declaration of the preeminence of Jesus and outlines the specific blessings we receive when we place our faith in Him. It begins like this:

> Paul, an apostle of Christ Jesus by the will of God, to God's holy people in Ephesus, the faithful in Christ Jesus: Grace and peace to you from God our Father and the Lord Jesus Christ. Praise be to the God and Father of our Lord Jesus Christ, who has blessed us in the heavenly realms with *every spiritual blessing* in Christ. For he *chose us* in him before the creation of the world to be holy and blameless in his sight. In *love* he predestined us for *adoption* to sonship through Jesus Christ, in accordance with his pleasure and will—to the praise of his glorious grace, which he has freely given us in the One he loves. (Ephesians 1:1–6)

Paul opens this letter with a common introduction identifying himself as the sender and "God's holy people in Ephesus" as the recipients. "Holy people" simply means those who are set apart for God, those who have trusted Christ, those who have entered by faith into His purposes for His people. So, as broad as this letter is in its implications, it is not directed toward everyone. It is written to those who have believed. Everything we will discuss in the coming pages is specifically for those who are in Christ.

In verse 3, Paul begins what is the longest sentence in the New Testament in the original Greek, a string of amazing thoughts that take us on a journey through spiritual blessings. Paul's point is right at the beginning of these thoughts: God "has blessed us in the heavenly realms with every spiritual blessing in Christ." If you are part of God's family, you already have all of these blessings. You may not have learned how to experience them yet. You may not have even accepted the fact that you have them.

But they are yours.

Chosen by God

The first spiritual blessing Paul mentions is this: *We are chosen by God.*

In fact, every spiritual blessing begins with this truth. He wants you. You were not an accident; you did not come into His family as an intruder or an unworthy visitor. You were handpicked by God for a relationship with Him.

In the suburban neighborhood where I grew up, the kids would play football on the lawns between the driveways. We played tackle football, so it helped to be big, which I wasn't. I was a few years younger than most, and I was small and skinny. So, when team captains picked sides, I was usually among the last two or three players to be chosen. I'd promise anything to get chosen: "I'll dive on the concrete. I'll make the bigger kids laugh. I'll run all the assignments no one else wants to run." I'd do whatever. I just wanted to be on the team. I wanted to belong.

That's everyone's desire, isn't it? The teams and circumstances change over the years, but we still want to be included.

You were handpicked by God for a relationship with Him.

We want to be in a club or organization; get initiated as a member of a fraternity, sorority, or gang; be accepted into the popular group of friends; get invited to the fun parties; or be welcomed into the neighborhood. So, we position ourselves for belonging—the fashions that look cool, the body or bank account that raises eyebrows, the achievements that impress, the professions that are admired, and so on. We do a lot of crazy things to belong to one group or another. We all desperately want to be wanted.

Several key points about being chosen stand out in Ephesians 1:4 that speak to our deep desire to be wanted.

For one thing, our chosen-ness is not based on our merit. We did nothing to earn it; it's based on what Christ did, not on what we do. Second, it's eternal. We were chosen from before the creation of the world. And finally, notice the purpose clause: We are chosen *in order that* we might be holy and blameless in God's sight. In other words, *we are wanted.* He "wants everyone to be saved and to understand the truth" (1 Tim. 2:4 NLT).

The things we used to do to make ourselves appealing and desirable are no longer necessary, at least not in any eternally meaningful sense. We may still write our résumé with a certain position in mind or dress ourselves appropriately for certain events and relationships, but we don't have to do anything to make ourselves wanted by God.

Most of our lives have been filled with a lot of *if*s: If I could do this; if I could achieve that; if I could look this way or have that thing or be more likable; and on and on. The implication of all these ifs is that our acceptance is conditional, a matter of making ourselves look, act, think, feel, or work more acceptably so we can actually be accepted. But in Christ, our inner longing and hardwiring to be wanted has been satisfied.

Do you know what that means? So many of us have made decisions, large or small, based on our need to be wanted. We may not be aware of the running commentary in our minds that leads us into unhealthy choices, but it's there, and it has devastating consequences: "I don't really want to go to bed with him or her, but I'm afraid I'll lose the relationship if I don't. I don't want to spend every weekend following my children all over the state, but I'm afraid they won't be accepted by their friends if they aren't on the traveling team. I don't feel like this is the right job for me, but I'm afraid no one else will want me if I turn it down." This line of thinking can take a multitude of forms, sometimes with insignificant decisions and sometimes with major life-altering ones. But in every case, it is based on our deep-seated need to be wanted and accepted.

Can you imagine what it would look like for all of those issues to be resolved? What would it feel like to eliminate all those things you consciously and unconsciously do to be wanted? What if all that positioning, posturing, and prep work became unnecessary? What if all those things you wanted and *needed* really aren't needed anymore? What if you were deeply, thoroughly, irrevocably convinced that you are so wanted and loved by the One who made you that you never needed to prove anything to anyone again?

What if you could finally say, "I don't have to work seventy hours a week anymore. I don't have to keep up with my coworkers or my neighbors. My kids don't have to get into the right school. I don't have to drive the right car, and we don't have to live in the right neighborhood." If those things happen, great. If not, no big deal. Your value is no longer at stake, and you're at peace in the depths of your soul, because what other people think no longer controls your thoughts and actions. The only thing that matters is what God thinks, and He has already made that clear. You are chosen, desired, wanted, and deeply valued just for who you are in Christ.

> *You are chosen, desired, wanted, and deeply valued just for who you are in Christ.*

Sounds wonderful, doesn't it? Yet this freedom from the disease of a high-maintenance self-image is still elusive for so many of us. How can we break it?

The answer is found in Ephesians chapter 1, verse 4, which tells us we are chosen by God, and verse 5 tells us the purpose we were chosen: "In love he predestined us for *adoption to sonship* through Jesus Christ, in accordance with his pleasure and will" (Ephesians 1:4b–5). So not only did God pick us out for Himself personally; He has adopted us, which means that we are complete in Him with all the rights and privileges of being in His family. This is an irrevocable relationship. Once you are adopted into God's family, you are related to Him forever. You are not only accepted by God, you are His child.

I can tell you from my own experience that this truth penetrates our minds easily but sinks into our hearts very slowly and with great difficulty. Perhaps it seems too good to be true, or maybe it just seems to contradict a lifetime of experience.

Let me ask you a personal and pointed question: Are you still living like a spiritual orphan? Your instinct may be to say no, but think about it.

Do you know in your head that you are loved by God while in your heart you are still looking for love everywhere else? Are you driven to succeed in order to feel like you are valued or worthwhile? Are you hypersensitive to criticism because it feels so much like rejection? Do you sabotage relationships or avoid them so you won't be at risk of rejection? Do you feel as if you need to please everyone so no one will reject you? Are you putting God on hold while all your energy goes into gaining approval and acceptance for your achievements, your insights, your reputation, or something else?

If the answer to some of those questions is yes, then let me help you explore the real meaning of adoption. As someone who has struggled deeply with pleasing people, the doctrine of adoption has been transformative for me. It's only when we come to understand the biblical concept of adoption that we can grasp what it means to be in Christ.

But before we get into that, we need to understand that the concept of adoption had a specific—and startling—meaning to the people who first received this letter.

The Real Meaning of Adoption

I had the privilege of adopting Theresa's two boys shortly after we were married. For anyone who has adopted children or been adopted, Ephesians 1 carries a lot of weight. But if you were in Ephesus when Paul's letter was read to the churches in the area, your understanding of adoption would be different from our modern experiences.

In Roman law, adoption applied mainly to adults. Occasionally a relative would adopt children whose parents had died, but more often adoption meant designating an heir to the family fortune for someone with no natural heirs. An appropriate adoptee would be identified, usually the brightest and best the person could find, and he, or sometimes she, would legally become the son, or daughter, and heir.

Perhaps the most famous example of this kind of adoption was Julius Caesar's adoption of his great-nephew, Octavian, who would later become the emperor Augustus. Late in his reign, Augustus did the same with a stepson and former son-in-law, Tiberius, who then became emperor. Very often, an adopted heir would be in his twenties or thirties at the time of adoption, and once adopted, his past would essentially be rewritten to reflect his new identity. His old debts would be paid in full, his legal obligations would vanish, and his name would be changed to that of his new family. But it was always very clear that this adoptee was chosen for his merit—his potential to invest and increase the family fortune and to honor the family name. The adoptee had to be worthy.

A first-century Christian reading Ephesians 1 would be astounded at the idea of God adopting unworthy human beings. A wealthy Roman citizen might adopt someone with a lot of potential, but the God of the universe adopting ordinary people and making us His heirs? That's a practice most people would never dream of or understand.

When one of my sons went through a time of rebellion, I remember coming to the end of my rope (and his!) and having to tell him, with tears streaming down my face, how we couldn't continue doing life the way we had been. "You've got a couple of days to decide whether you can keep living in our home or not. If you're old enough to do whatever you want, maybe you need to go do that somewhere else. It would break our heart, and we will never stop loving you, but we don't know what else to do."

By God's grace, my son did an about-face. Like many young people, he had gone through some genuine doubts about the reality of God, and a lot of those doubts had shown up as resistance to what he had been taught. After our talk, he went into his bedroom for a couple of days and pondered deeply what he was going to do. He reengaged with God and God met him powerfully. He came back out and began to walk with God in a new way. The change was so dramatic that I had to ask, "Son, what happened?"

It wasn't one of my penetrating sermons that changed his heart. In fact, it wasn't anything I would have expected. In a moment of intimacy, vulnerability, and tenderness, he said, "Dad, I've doubted everything you believe, and I'm sure part of that was being a kid in a big church where people put a lot of pressure on our family. I had a hard time handling it, and I knew I was rebelling. But I spent two days thinking about how real Jesus is to you and Mom."

He went on to explain how Theresa and I hadn't pressured him to behave a certain way in order to maintain our reputation at church. "You're the same people at home as you are there," he said. "I see you and Mom pray, and I'm not sure about the things I'm doubting, but God sure is real to you. I just asked Him to help me like never before—to be real to me."

I believe the reason we are losing our youth is not only the things they hear at college or in the media. That's difficult, of course, but culture has always been challenging for Christians. What they need to see is the reality of life with the Father—not only dropping them off at church, but the depths of a real relationship with God. They need to see a heart that beats for God—not merely a commitment to moral principles, but people who cry over their sin, who bear each other's burdens, and who live authentically with their heavenly Father.

It was not programs or rules that changed my son's life. It was his intimate encounter with the living God.

How to See Yourself as God Sees You

Plenty of theologians are well versed in the truths of God's love and His adoption of His children. But that knowledge alone does not change lives. It doesn't keep us from seeking love and approval for reasons we can't quite put our finger on. Our need for belonging and the issues that keep us from experiencing it run really deep.

How do we get these wonderful truths to take that eighteen-inch journey from our heads to our hearts?

First, we have to replace our warped mirrors, our false beliefs about ourselves, with the truth of God's Word. I described one of the best ways to do that in the last chapter when I explained the index cards Theresa and I used daily to reshape and renew our minds to think in new ways. We identified the lies we believed, and we wrote each one on a three-by-five-inch index card. On the other side of each card, we wrote the corresponding truth along with a Bible verse that confirmed it. Then we read each card slowly every morning and most nights for about two years.

These cards became tools that allowed that eighteen-inch journey to occur. We have shared them informally with others for years and have watched God do for others what He did in us. In recent days, Living on the Edge printed them, and now thousands of people use them. The principle is simple and the impact amazing: we replace the warped mirrors of our lives with the truth of Scripture.

I vividly remember watching my wife go through a series of these cards with my daughter for three or four years during those crucial teenage years. Like all teens, she struggled with the lies of the culture and with physical insecurities. Yet, by her renewing her mind, I now have a daughter who knows she is wanted, appreciated, and loved by God—the most important person in her life. She has made some very courageous and difficult decisions under peer pressure because she knew in her heart who she really is and that she belongs to God.

As you review these lies and the truths that correct them, you may begin to notice that some of the ways you have been

Misbelief

- I must be approved or accepted by certain people in order to be happy.

- I need other people's affirmation to know I am wanted.

Truth

I am wanted, appreciated, and loved by God, the most important person in my life.

"For he chose us in him before the creation of the world to be holy and blameless in his sight."
Ephesians 1:4

making decisions about your life, work, and relationships are rooted in the need for approval. You may become more aware of your insecurities. But the truth of belonging to God and being wanted by Him will gradually sink into your heart, and something wonderful and strange will happen deep inside. You will begin to see life differently. You will see your need to perform and gain others' approval gradually dissipate. You will, over time, actually discover your true self.

A word of caution: this is not a magical fix. But if you do this consistently for several months, you will notice significant, progressive changes in your beliefs and relationships.

You will begin to live like a son or daughter of God. You will find yourself reading the Bible, not because you have to, but because you want to. You will pray longer, not because you're supposed to, but because you enjoy spending time with your Father. You will begin to respond to others differently and feel less compelled to accommodate them just to avoid rejection. In other words, you will know who you are, and you will know that you are wanted. You have been chosen, and you are adopted by a Father who will never reject you.

Questions for Reflection and Discussion

1) Think of a time you tried out for a team. What was the team? Were you chosen? Did you find yourself positioning for belonging? In what ways?

2) We live in a world of conditional ifs, and life decisions, whether subconsciously or consciously, are often made based on the need to be wanted. How have you seen this lived out in the world around you? How has this played out in your own life?

3) Most of us can agree that we live like spiritual orphans at times. We know in our minds that we are loved by God, while in our hearts we are looking for love somewhere else. What tangible substitutes for God's love have you pursued or are you pursuing?

4) How is our modern context of adoption similar to and how is it different from adoption according to Roman law? Does it change the way you see yourself as adopted by God? Why or why not?

5) Which of the five adoption truths, listed below, stands out to you the most? Why?

- When you are adopted, you are loved.
- When you are adopted, you have hope.
- When you are adopted, you have intimacy.
- When you are adopted, you seek holiness.
- When you understand adoption, you have assurance.

6) Write down these thoughts and post them where you can see them throughout the day: *God chose me. God wants me. God loves me.* Every time you come across these truths, read them slowly and aloud. Let the truth of Ephesians 1:4 soak into your heart and ask for God's help in this.

PART 2

VALUABLE

3

The Lie of Insignificance

Like many immigrants, my friend David's parents came to America so their children could have a better life. They left behind a harsh and threatening situation in Southeast Asia, took menial jobs, and worked hard at learning a new language. Their small family business struggled at first, but with long hours and a relentless desire to forge a new beginning, their "better life" began to take root.

David's parents, especially his mother, saw education as the key to a better life. "We did extra homework," he says. "We couldn't just get A's. We had to get better than A's." Even though his parents worked day and night, they devoted much of their time to pushing their children to do better. They sacrificed their own interests for their children's education.

When David was still in the third grade, he began studying five or six hours every Saturday for the SAT and ACT. He got one break per week for a couple hours. "My mom thought we needed to get to know American culture, and there was a church nearby. It was an evangelical, Bible-teaching congregation with a youth group. She would drop us off between studies."

David didn't see this new life the way his parents did. He and his siblings felt torn between two worlds. They wanted to be accepted, yet they had to spend most of their time studying while their friends were involved in other activities and having fun. They got one message from American culture, another from their parents. They felt loved only when they excelled in school and in their careers. It was imperative for them to get into a prestigious university and land a prestigious job. The message was clear. David's parents' love and acceptance were based on his performance.

Understanding Significance and Value

As a result of their family's emphasis on performance, David's sister got a perfect score on her college entrance exams, went to an Ivy League university for her undergraduate and graduate degrees, and ultimately ended up with a great job . . . and no relationship with her family. She changed her address multiple times so her mother couldn't contact her. She lived her entire life under the pressure of a lie: that a person's value, validation, and even reason for existence are to excel. But no matter how much she did, it was never enough. To this day, she cannot bear to be around her mother. Her mom produced a very successful daughter but lost her in the process.

We all have a God-given need to know that we matter, that we are valuable and worthwhile. Our parents are the first people in our lives to help us meet those deep needs. Some parents make it really clear that love and value are unconditional; others convey another message. But no parent is perfect, and society reinforces a lot of skewed messages throughout the course of our lives. As a result, we all come away with distorted perspectives about our own significance.

This is where many of our lifelong struggles and addictions come from. As much as we may think that the fundamental issue in our lives is our behaviors, and as much as we focus on changing them, the real issue goes much deeper. It isn't about habits or dysfunctional relationships. Those are symptoms of a bigger problem: our distorted understanding of our own significance and value.

Our Search for Significance

In his classic book, *The Search for Significance,* Robert McGee wrote:

> From life's onset, we find ourselves searching to satisfy some inner unexplained yearning. Our hunger causes us to search for people who will love us. Our desire for acceptance pressures us to perform for the praise of others. Our desire to be loved and accepted is a symptom of our deeper need."

That underlying need, McGee says, governs our behavior and is the source of our emotional pain, yet few people even recognize it. It's our need for self-worth.[1]

In fact, McGee says the real problem is that since our separation from God, human beings have failed to turn to Him to find out the truth about ourselves. Instead, we look to others: parents, peers, mates, and other important people in our lives. We reason that what others say about us is true and that we will find our value in living up to their standards and expectations.

That's why so many people who have heard distorted messages about their self-worth spend a lifetime trying to find themselves or prove their worth, and it's why so many people keep running after whatever popular culture says is "cool" or "in." Every single one of us has been imprinted with a formula that says our self-worth comes from our performance and others' opinions.

SELF-WORTH = PERFORMANCE + OTHERS' OPINIONS

This formula is so deeply ingrained in us that we find ourselves powerfully drawn to addictions and habits we learned early in life. Our behaviors are unintentional answers to questions we are constantly asking ourselves: "Am I good at this? Do people like me? Am I pretty/handsome? Am I popular/funny/smart? Am I accepted?" Few of us realize it, but much of what we do is an effort to prove our significance, to show that we are important, valuable, competent, or accepted.

Different cultures and families come up with different ways to answer these questions, but the human race as a whole has been brainwashed to believe our significance is not found in who we are but in what we do and what others think about us. We are on a universal search to answer a universal question: Am I worth it?

Where Do You Seek Identity Apart from Christ?

I've met countless Christians who are theologically astute but who are driven by deep unmet needs that go back to their childhood. Until we meet Jesus—and very often afterward—we habitually put our identity in other things and other people. I've found that most people, including me, who know the right answers, still have some strong, unhealthy motives driving them.

Most people, including me, who know the right answers, still have some strong, unhealthy motives driving them.

Let me ask you: Where do you tend to look for your significance? Every one of us has looked for our identity in something or someone other than Jesus. What are those things for you?

I have a pretty long list, and I've realized that there is almost no limit to the ways we seek validation. As you read through the possibilities below—and it is admittedly a partial list—see which ones resonate with you.

- Success—careers, achievements, awards, promotions, positions (or raising children who have great careers, achievements, etc.)
- Education—the letters after your name or the skills you've acquired

- Money—security in your bank account or the status wealth can give you
- Possessions—surrounding yourself with valuables or getting a rush from acquiring new things
- Image/reputation—styles, fashions, or trends you follow; being a great dad, mom, partner, friend; having people look up to you for admirable traits like integrity or morality
- Personal characteristics—being funny, smart, popular, quirky, extravagant, sophisticated, honest, sacrificial, needy, self-sufficient, etc.
- Relationships—finding identity in having the right friends, spouse, etc.
- Popularity—being recognized in a certain group or on social media
- Ministry—being identified for service to God, sacrifice, dedication, fruitfulness

You'll notice that none of these things is bad in itself, right? There's nothing wrong with accomplishments, a great reputation, serving God, being funny or smart, having wealth, being educated, or being liked. These are great goals to strive for. But if they become the basis of your identity, something is terribly wrong. You will find yourself chasing a vision you can never fulfill.

These things will never tell you who you really are.

Understanding *Your* Search for Significance

This search for identity is closely related to the search for significance, because we can't know how valuable we are until we know who we are. We all fall back on looking for our identity in certain people or things from time to time. Breaking out of this trap of performing to gain people's approval demands that we learn to identify our default patterns.

Our attempts to meet our needs for success and approval fall into two broad categories: compulsion and withdrawal. You'll probably find that you do some of both. But if you're like most people, you will tend to lean strongly in one direction or the other.

> *We can't know how valuable we are until we know who we are.*

Compulsion. Those of us who seek our identity in compulsion tend to be perfectionistic. We are driven to succeed, which can make us prone to workaholism, being obsessed with outward appearance, or manipulating and using people for personal achievement. I can identify with some aspects of that description. I was a workaholic by the time I was twelve. To this day, I still worry too much about what people think, am driven toward success, and find myself tempted daily to seek people's approval. I'm not nearly as bad about that as I used to be, but, in weak moments, that's my default. My tendency is to be compulsive.

Withdrawal. We generally marry people who default to the other category, and that's true for Theresa and me. She's a withdrawer. Those of us who withdraw avoid failure, avoid risk, and gravitate toward others who are comforting and kind, or even needy—anyone "safe." We avoid relationships that demand vulnerability. We may appear easygoing but often run from potential situations or relationships that might not succeed.

If you look carefully, you'll notice that both of these responses are prompted by a fear of rejection and a fear of failure. The goal is either to prove to people that we are significant and valuable so that we are not rejected as failures, or to protect ourselves from the appearance or possibility that we are failures. And these fears will stay with us, at some level, for the rest of our lives, either as very present problems or latent possibilities. We are always aware of the potential of rejection and failure.

Even though these two tendencies—compulsion and withdrawal—are very different and manifest in unique ways, the result is the same: we become slaves.

We are captive to other people's opinions. We make decisions according to the expectations of those around us. This starts very early—with a father and/or mother who tell us what we're like, how we're gifted, what we're supposed to do in life, and what behaviors win the most affection from them—but our captivity to others' opinions can continue throughout our whole lives.

We start living for someone else. We start defining ourselves by labels others apply to us: whether a certain clique tells us we're in or out, whether a school's acceptance committee thinks we're smart or dumb, whether a popular guy or girl thinks we're attractive or not, and so on. Somewhere deep inside, we decide we're fast, slow, dumb, smart, good, bad, funny, weird, or whatever.

If we aren't careful, we might live out the rest of our days either fulfilling those labels or trying to prove it isn't true. We may compulsively try to live up to the standard or defy it, or we might withdraw from anyone who might confirm or deny it for us. In any case, we are captive to the opinions of others.

As a result, we unconsciously become actors. Our inner antennas go up, our radar searches the responses around us, and we figure out what works. We may do it with different groups in different seasons of our lives, but we all do it. You can observe little children working this out. *When I say this, I get approval. When I say that, I don't. When I dress like this, people like me. When I dress like that, they think I don't fit in. When I achieve this, parents and teachers think I'm special, and my peers get jealous, and now I have to choose whose opinion matters.*

Over time, instead of becoming your true self, you become a slave to what other people think, the terms they dictate, and the roles they expect you to play.

I've experienced this in different ways at different times in my life, but I especially remember the dramatic change that occurred after I received the gospel. Prior to receiving Christ, I had always been willing to change my behavior or play the role that was required by the group I was interacting with. I cussed like a sailor in the locker room to gain the tough-guy standing with other team members. Around coaches and other adults, I was the all-American boy. I figured out what each group wanted, and I played that role. I was a phony, a hypocrite, and a chameleon.

Needless to say, I didn't like myself. I wondered, *Who am I, really?*

But shortly after receiving Christ, I experienced a new freedom. Though my role-playing for approval didn't entirely change as soon as I received Christ, I was now aware of it. I realized it didn't have to be that way. I began a journey of learning how to be my true self.

As long as you are acting, however, your true self is never seen. And because your true self is never seen, your true self is never loved. Some people have never seen your true self. In fact, you may not even know who the true self inside you actually is. For many of us, it takes years, even decades, to sort out the different roles we've played and then discover who we really are.

Virtually all of us, then, have never been fully seen for who we really are and, more tragically, have never been loved for who we really are. We've received affirmation, to be sure, but that is not the same thing as receiving love. We may get good grades at school, be commended for being responsible adults, receive accolades for accomplishing something great, get promoted for our workaholism, and get all sorts of other kudos and affirmations. But that is not love.

If those things have become our identity, we might mistake them for love, when what we have is a dysfunctional behavioral pattern that never satisfies. It keeps us working hard and craving even more affirmation, but it's never enough. We may receive a lot of praise for the image we project, but deep down, we know it isn't directed at the true person inside. Even when people say they love us, the love doesn't penetrate deep into our hearts, because we know they don't know who we really are.

Every single person desperately craves authentic acceptance—someone to see through our exterior to the good, bad, and ugly inside, and accept and love us in spite of what they see.

Virtually all of us, then, have never been fully seen for who we really are and, more tragically, have never been loved for who we really are.

We may be blessed to get that from some significant people in our lives, but the first person we need to look to is God. God has created billions of people, each with unique DNA and unique combinations of abilities, physical attributes, personality traits, gifts, and talents. He loves each one of us. He doesn't love us for what we have done. But like a parent holding a newborn, He loved us before we could do anything at all. So, He is not looking for people who can imitate someone else or fit some mold that is different from His original design for us. He simply loves us as He has made us.

The most beautiful, liberating thing that can happen to us is to realize that God made us the way we are for a reason and we have no need to be anything or anyone else. We are free to say no to the lies. When we do, we grow into our unique selves and become very attractive simply for who we are. That's God's design for us.

The story of my friend David's family that began this chapter ended bitterly for his sister. But something happened to David at the youth group he attended all those Saturdays when he was dropped off to learn about American culture. He was accepted. He felt loved. He had never opened a Bible before, but he began to read it and get God's picture of him. He entered into a relationship with Jesus, and, little by little, the lies began to fade. He came to realize that even though school and grades were important, they were not what defined him. He certainly did well in school and in his career, but far more important was his relationship with God. He found his significance there as one who is truly loved, accepted, and valued.

Unlike his sister, David was eventually able to leave behind his resentment, forgive his mother, look past her standards, and see her motives. She wanted the best for her children, but she was misguided in how to give it to them. David has chosen not to believe the lie that he can only be valued and accepted by living up to an impossible standard. In fact, he now leads groups that go around the world helping people discover who they really are. He even serves in Southeast Asia, the part of the world his parents came from. David's story is a beautiful one, a story of learning how to not only identify the lies but overcome them with truth.

We all struggle—even as mature believers—with our search for significance. Left to ourselves we become the prisoners of other people's opinions, slaves to performance, and actors in search of ourselves. Thanks be to God for Jesus's promise that we can abide in the truth and the truth will set us free (John 8:32).

Questions for Reflection and Discussion

1) How would the "American dream" or popular culture define a successful life? Do you agree with these definitions of success? How would you define a successful life?

2) Do you relate to this formula?
   Self-Worth = Performance + Others' Opinions
   How has this formula impacted your life?

3) There are many ways we seek validation and find our significance. Circle any of the areas in which you have sought to find your value.

   Success
   Education
   Money
   Possessions
   Image/Reputation
   Personal Characteristics
   Relationships
   Popularity
   Ministry
   Other: _____

4) Have you noticed that when these ways become first in our hearts, they eventually seem to disappoint and not satisfy? Why do you think that is?

5) In his book *Mere Christianity*, C. S. Lewis writes, "If we find ourselves with a desire that nothing in this

world can satisfy, the most probable explanation is that we were not made for this world."[2] What insight does Lewis add to this discussion?

6) In what areas of your life do you find yourself acting rather than being the real you? With whom are you free to be the real you? Write that person a card or take them to coffee and tell them what they mean to you.

4

You Are Valuable

Ephesians 1:7–10

Despite her sharp mind, good looks, and many friends, Theresa felt unworthy and unimportant. No matter how many compliments I gave her or how kindly I tried to treat her, my words and actions bounced off her like light off a mirror. I saw a beautiful, kind, and godly woman with whom I was head over heels in love. When she looked in the mirror, Theresa saw an ugly woman who was worth nothing.

It was a long and at times painful journey in which we *both* desperately needed to learn to see ourselves as new creations in Christ rather than through the brokenness of our backgrounds. Her challenge was to overcome rejection and a sense of worthlessness. Mine was to stop trying to prove my value and worthiness by my overachieving and workaholic performance.

Somewhere along our journey, something clicked in me that helped us both. Although I didn't know much theology at the time, I remember God speaking to me through a verse. Something Paul wrote helped me take a vague idea that God valued me into a concrete concept that we could get our arms and heads around.

> Do you not know that your body is a temple of the Holy Spirit who is in you, whom you have from God and that you are not your own? For you have been bought with a price: therefore honor God in your body. (1 Cor. 6:19–20 NASB)

It was the phrase "you have been bought with a price" that began to take me from wishful thinking to logical reality. I remember thinking, *Theresa may not think she's worth very much; but God thinks she's worth the ultimate price He could pay to redeem her: the very death of His Son. I may not think I'm worth much unless I excel in every area of my life, but God thought I was worth the death of His Son, the purchase price to redeem me.*

Imagine a box floating in front of you. We'll call it box number one. Right next to it is a box exactly the same size and color. Let's call it box number two. The only difference between the two boxes is that box number one has a price tag on it of $1,000 and box number two has a price tag of $1,000,000. You don't know what's inside each of those boxes, but you do know their relative worth. There's a big difference between $1,000 and $1,000,000.

If you were on a game show, and you were told to pick between box number one and box number two without knowing the contents—but with the assurance that the price marked on the front was accurate—you wouldn't have much difficulty deciding. It doesn't take a genius to figure out that if something costs more, it's worth more. The cost of something may not always be an exact reflection of its value, but cost and value are certainly related. If a well-off man proposes with a ring that costs thirty dollars, it's a different statement than proposing with a ring that costs $3,000. When something costs a lot—when the sacrifice for it is big—that tells us something about its value.

You and I cost a lot. God made an extraordinary sacrifice for our redemption. We know we are worth a lot to Him, because we cost Him the precious blood of His Son. That means we have infinite value in His eyes. Regardless of whatever problems, struggles, challenges, pains, and wounds you've experienced, regardless of what lies you've believed, and regardless of how you happen to feel about yourself at the moment, you are worth the blood of Christ. God sent His perfect Son from heaven into a world that would ridicule, torment, and kill Him for the sake of sinners. There is no greater statement of value than that. That's how much we matter.

> *We know we are worth a lot to Him, because we cost Him the precious blood of His Son. That means we have infinite value in His eyes.*

Your relationship with God does not end with being chosen and adopted; you are also redeemed. Ephesians goes on to say, "In him we have redemption through his blood, the forgiveness of sins, in accordance with the riches of God's grace that he lavished on us" (Eph. 1:7–8).

Redemption is a theologically heavy word, but it simply means that you have been purchased by God and are His infinitely precious and treasured possession. It is the complete opposite of being loved and valued only for what you can do or how you look. Redemption is not about your performance, nor does it have anything to do with other people's approval. Only your heavenly Father's opinion matters.

That does not mean we have to deny that other people's opinions matter to us. Approval can be nice. Most of us crave it. But as you grow more and more secure in your Father's love, you don't *have* to have it. Your approval comes from a much greater source than maintaining a certain lifestyle or image. If your status and validation are already irrevocably secured by the only One who matters, approval becomes a nice addition, not a necessity. As human beings, compliments and praise are music to our ears. We all love them, but they do not define us.

If you want this reality to move from your head to your heart, you must learn how to tell yourself the truth. It even helps to say it out loud to yourself again and again: "I am the precious treasure of my heavenly Father. I am loved and valued forever. My future is not dependent on what anyone else thinks, what anyone else does, or what anyone else says is cool or right or wonderful. I am holy, beloved, blessed with every spiritual blessing, chosen, and adopted. I've been redeemed."

What Does It Mean to Be Redeemed?

How have we been redeemed? Through the blood of Jesus. Redemption is the forgiveness of our trespasses, a pardon for all those times we knew the right thing to do and crossed the line anyway. We are redeemed according to "the riches of God's grace that he lavished on us" (Ephesians 1:7).

If we lived in first-century Ephesus and heard these words about our redemption, we would immediately think of the agora, the central marketplace. Every agora had a small platform where slaves were bought and sold. People could go there to buy a man, a woman, a child, or even a whole family to serve in their home, business, or fields. Paul is using this vocabulary in Ephesians 1 to portray our redemption as a purchase—the price God has paid to redeem us from our enslavement to sin and death and to set us free.

Our freedom came at an enormous cost because of our immense value to God. We dare not reject it or waste it. As Paul puts it in another letter, "It is for freedom that Christ has set us free" (Galatians 5:1). God purchased us from the slave market of sin at the cost of Jesus's human life, and He made us His infinitely precious and treasured possession, because He loves us.

Can you imagine how differently you would see yourself if you actually believed that the Creator of the universe paid such an extravagant price for you?

Your True Self Is Free and Valuable

Every single person on the face of the earth—you and I and everyone we know—has been caught up in the slave market of sin. It's a relentless captivity. We know the right thing to do and don't do it. We commit sin by doing the wrong things and by neglecting the right things. We don't always intend to live this way, but every generation has inherited these tendencies. Sinfulness is our default nature outside of Christ, which explains why our attempts to do the right thing often make us feel as if we are swimming against the tide.

Paul and other biblical writers describe this fallen nature in terms of captivity, and when Jesus came and died on the cross for us, He atoned for our sins. Literally, He ransomed us. He paid the purchase price of our salvation and freedom with His own life.

> *In the central marketplace of this universe, God bought us off the platform of slavery with the purchase price of the death of His Son.*

In the central marketplace of this universe, God bought us off the platform of slavery with the purchase price of the death of His Son.

That's how much we're worth. The blood of His Son is of infinite value, so God paid an infinite price. No matter what people have said about you, no matter what feelings and struggles and pain you have experienced, no matter what lies you have believed, you are worth the blood of Jesus. The perfect Son of God left heaven and lived a life of love for sinful people who matter more than any of us can imagine.

As you start believing that you are chosen, adopted, and redeemed, you will progressively take on a new identity. You will begin to embrace the message that your true self in Christ is free and valuable, even if you have felt just the opposite. You will learn to walk in extreme gratitude toward

God and have confidence in His purposes for your life. You will little by little become who you were created and designed to be.

When I teach this truth, I often hear a lot of emotional objections, even from people who accept it theologically: "You don't understand, Chip. I had a very difficult childhood." Or, "It's a nice ideal, but life hasn't worked out that way for me." Or, "I've believed in Jesus for a long time, and I still feel the pain of all the ways I've been wounded in the past."

Though all of those objections come from real feelings and authentic experiences, they are not the ultimate truth. They don't trump God's verdict about your identity. They describe the distortions that have come, not the original design and purpose you were given. It's true that life can be hard, that sin is real, and that people have done wrong to you.

But what defines you? Is it all of those experiences or the *truth* that God declares above them? God's opinion of you is reality. If you want to know your true self, you must anchor yourself in His Word.

Radical transformations take time and require an intentional, systematic process. This is a journey for all of us, an ongoing, replenishing process of identifying the lies, calling them what they are, and replacing them with truth. The more we engage in this process, the more the truth sinks into our hearts. Mental assent is just the beginning; we change when the truth affects us emotionally and works its way out in our words and actions. Over time, our new identity feels like a perfect fit.

I know that, because the woman I married doesn't exist anymore. Her shattered self-image and negative thoughts have been replaced by a woman who sees herself as precious in God's sight. Over the years, it's been like watching a flower unfold. I'm here to tell you that this is God's plan for you too.

Your True Self Is Needed and Worthy

At some point in our lives, most of us ask some big questions: *Who am I? Why am I here? What is the meaning of life?*

Perhaps you have achieved all of your goals and realize something is still missing. *There has to be more to life than having money and the perfect house and a vacation home and connections with powerful people and . . .*

Or maybe you feel like a failure, because you've tried everything you know to make life meaningful, but nothing has worked. If you've ever been there, you need to know that you are not only redeemed, but you are redeemed for a purpose:

> In all wisdom and insight He made known to us the mystery of His will, according to His kind intention which He purposed in Him with a view to an administration suitable to the fullness of the times, that is, the summing up of all things in Christ, things in the heavens and things on the earth. (Ephesians 1:8–10 NASB)

This whole sentence reflects the definition of our redemption. Paul calls it a "mystery," which means only that it had been secret, a part of God's will that was not known until the revelation of Jesus and our salvation. He did this "according to His kind intention," which means our redemption is not another kind of slavery to the law or to impossible demands but for the purpose of having a meaningful, fulfilling relationship with Jesus. And the language Paul uses for how God put it into effect at the right time refers to the rules and management of His household—literally the economy of His home.

Just as we have a family budget, bedtimes for our kids, and chores for every member to carry out in order to fulfill family goals, God has a purpose and plan for the management of His family as well. He brought about our redemption and our adoption to fulfill that purpose and plan. And He revealed the mystery of redemption through Jesus *at the right time* for the sake of His kingdom, the family business. Here Paul is referring to *kairos* time, a unique moment of opportunity. This unique fulfillment of time is a summing up of all things in Christ, bringing unity to everything under heaven.

In other words, you are an important part of God's big plan.

The central theme of this redemption plan is the church—those who believe in Jesus, both Jew and Gentile. This brand-new family is under a new covenant as the spiritual body of Jesus. Just as Jesus displayed the nature and character of the Father, loved extravagantly, healed the sick, fed the hungry, and demonstrated what it means to be salt and light in the world, so have we been called to do all of these things as we are conformed into the image of Jesus.

You have not been called to pursue your own happiness. You're now a part of the family of God, filled with His Spirit, carrying His nature, and walking out His mission as the very

Valuable

body of Christ. In a world that desperately needs Him, you are an indispensable agent of love and mercy.

So you see, God redeemed you first and foremost because you are infinitely valued by Him, and second, to grant you the unspeakable privilege of being Jesus's agents of blessing in your everyday world, 24/7.

> *In a world that desperately needs Him, you are an indispensable agent of love and mercy.*

Your infinite value and God-given purpose are a reality regardless of your track record, background, job, social standing, IQ, or any other standard the world uses to measure your usefulness. Jesus is putting together a puzzle, a temple of living stones that fit together as a beautiful collage of the grace of God. You have become part of a supernatural mission to display Jesus so others can see His love. Every day, you have an opportunity to reflect Him so that family members, neighbors, coworkers, fellow church members, and the people who do business where you buy coffee, groceries, and everything else can see redemption in real life. His life, lived out through you, provides hope for others.

If you need any motivation to get up in the morning, there it is. There is no greater purpose, no stronger message from your Father to prove how important you are. Your true self is needed and worthy.

Knowing and believing that you're needed and worthy will change your life. We all need to be needed. Our self-esteem and sense of worth come not only from who we are but what we do. Our worthiness in God's kingdom is not about our performance or what anyone else thinks, it's about the calling we've been given and how we're able to contribute. In group Bible studies I've participated in, I've noticed that people tend to keep coming when they have something to contribute.

You've been given a priceless treasure and an invaluable calling. You're part of the family of God, and every person in His family is indispensable. Any sense of unworthiness or purposelessness is a lie. You've been made worthy through your redemption and given the eternal purpose of reflecting God's nature and demonstrating His love. You have not only been purchased from slavery but also given your freedom. You have been raised to a privileged position as a valuable, worthy, and very needed member of God's kingdom.

Replacing Misbeliefs with Statements of Truth

The best way to get these identity truths into our hearts is to replace our warped mirrors and beliefs with the truth of God's Word. Most of us carry plenty of misbeliefs about our own value, forgetting how much God sacrificed for our redemption and freedom. These misbeliefs generally fall into two categories:

MISBELIEFS

- *I must avoid failure at all costs. If I work harder and longer, then I will be a success and prove I'm not a failure.*

- *I must avoid failure at all costs. It's better not to try than to fail. If people truly get to know me, they would reject me.*

The first of these misbeliefs applies to compulsive people like me. If we're not careful, we get on a never-ending treadmill that keeps us running toward building our value but never getting anywhere.

The second applies to withdrawers who try to take themselves out of the equation before any evidence of unworthiness can come up. Those who withdraw get very upset when they make a mistake, because they assume others will be upset with them or think less of them. They fear the shame that comes from someone making fun of them.

Both compulsives and withdrawers are tempted to think that if they can't do something well, there's no point in doing it at all.

Misbeliefs like these drive us either to avoid risks or throw ourselves into them recklessly, to withhold our best efforts from those who would benefit from them or put forth our best efforts so relentlessly that we're never satisfied. Neither approach is healthy or satisfying.

What truth replaces these lies?

TRUTH

I am now a righteous person in God's sight since I have trusted Christ's redemptive sacrifice for me. I am covered by the robe of His purity and goodness. Also, since I have a new nature, I am a good person in my general practice of life as I continue to grow in Christ.

I recommend writing down this truth and then reading it over and over, thoughtfully and slowly. Think about how God accomplished this truth. Meditate on what it means for your life. Let it sink in.

As you do, you will begin to realize you are a righteous person in God's sight; you never need to earn His favor, and you can stop trying to impress everyone else. You will stop pursuing what God has said you already have.

Beware of the mental objections that might come up at this point. Your guilt and shame over past mistakes will quickly tell you, "You're not righteous." But if you look at yourself as God sees you, your past mistakes will become irrelevant. They are covered by the blood of Jesus. One of the most remarkable statements in the New Testament assures us of this: "God made him who had no sin to be sin for us, so that in him we might become the righteousness of God" (2 Cor. 5:21).

Do you believe that? *You have become the righteousness of God.* The moment you trusted Christ, God made a legal declaration that you were, and will always be, righteous in His eyes. You may not experience the fullness of that righteousness practically yet, at least not as much as you would like, but this is your legal position as far as He is concerned. As you begin to see yourself as God sees you, you will grow in your experience of His righteousness. His Spirit will be at work within you to change you from the inside out, and you will find yourself living out the change.

The first misbelief card below is the one Theresa and I reviewed years ago. The second card is one I wrote recently to help me continue to grow free of my people-pleasing tendency.

Misbelief

I must avoid failure at all costs. I must work harder and longer to be a success and prove I'm not a failure.

I must avoid failure at all costs. It's better not to try than to fail. If people really get to know me, they would reject me.

Truth

I am now a righteous person in God's sight since I have trusted Christ's redemptive sacrifice for me. I am also covered by a robe of His purity and goodness. Also, since I have a new nature, I am a good person in my central practice of life as I continue to grow in Christ.

"Therefore, if anyone is in Christ, the new creation has come: The old has gone, the new is here!"
2 Corinthians 5:17

Misbelief

I am a prisoner of the opinions of the important, influential people in my life. I apologize when my best judgment and direction from the Lord is different than theirs. Disagreeing with them will harm our relationship irreparably, so I attempt to please everyone, creating an unhealthy lifestyle.

Truth

People love me, are for me, and want me to live a life of joy, rhythm, rest, and fruitfulness in all areas of my life. I do not need to prove my worth through hard work or extraordinary productivity; I am accepted, loved, and greatly valued just for who I am.

"Am I now trying to win the approval of human beings, or of God? Or am I trying to please people? If I were still trying to please people, I would not be a servant of Christ."
Galatians 1:10

As members of our church began reviewing these truths and letting them sink into their hearts, I had people line up after services to tell me how much more they were experiencing God's love and acceptance. You too will realize how much God wants you to be able to live a life of joy, rest, and fruitfulness, and how much He has done to accomplish that life for you. And you will come to know, deep in your heart, that He values you just for who you are.

Questions for Reflection and Discussion

1) When the sacrifice is great, it speaks to the value of an item. Do you have something that is very valuable to you because the giver, out of a great love for you, sacrificed to give it to you?

2) How do you *know* that you are infinitely valuable to God and loved by Him? What was the price God paid for your freedom?

3) Not only are we chosen and adopted, we're redeemed. Paul says in Ephesians 1:7–8, "In him we have redemption through his blood, the forgiveness of sins, in accordance with the riches of God's grace that he lavished on us." According to this verse, how have we been redeemed?

4) In Galatians 5:1, Paul says, "It is for freedom that Christ has set us free." God purchased us out of sin's captivity into true freedom because He loves us dearly. Radical transformation takes time. One step in this long journey includes gratitude toward God. Take some time each day this week to thank Him for what He has done for you. Each day, write down five things He has done in your life that you are thankful for.

5) Which camp do you tend to fall into: the *withdrawers* or the *compulsives*? Why do you think so?

6) Create an index card or a digital version out of the Worthiness Truth and put it where you will see it

regularly. Read the truth slowly and aloud. Allow it to renew your mind and ask God for His help in replacing the lies with this truth.

Truth: I am now a righteous person in God's sight since I have trusted Christ's redemptive sacrifice for me. I am covered by the robe of His purity and goodness. Also, since I have a new nature, I am a good person in my general practice of life as I continue to grow in Christ.

PART 3

SECURE

5

The Lie of Fear

It was supposed to be just a second opinion. A few days at the prestigious Duke Medical Center to determine if there was some new treatment for the rare disease my mother was battling. Mom had brought an overnight bag from her home in Orlando, Florida, thinking the trip would be two or three days at the most. To our shock, my mom never left the hospital.

She was only sixty-two, full of life, energetic, the glue of our family, and, apart from my wife, my best friend.

Mom was the most emotionally intelligent person I've ever met. She was a counselor by profession and my counselor from afar. She had more than a sixth sense; God had gifted her with extraordinary discernment. It was Mom who sensed that God was moving me to marry Theresa (even before I said anything) and that I needed a word of encouragement to move forward—which she provided. She was a source of security, like all great moms are no matter how old we are.

At the time, I had been a pastor for about twelve years, but I wasn't prepared to walk into her hospital room and see her connected to so many tubes. She was so swollen that I didn't recognize her. I found a corner in the hospital, and I cried. As the days lingered before she was taken away from me, a foreboding sense of fear bombarded my soul and challenged my faith.

> *A foreboding sense of fear bombarded my soul and challenged my faith.*

In the wee hours of the morning, far from family and friends and alone with God, I wrestled with questions: *What do I really believe? Is heaven as certain as I've been taught—and have taught others? Who will I go to for counsel now?*

In my Bible next to Psalm 46, in green ink, it says "2/19/92 Duke Medical Center, Mom is dying." What that notation doesn't record is what God said to me when I read these words: "God is our refuge and strength, an ever-present help in trouble. Therefore we will not fear, though the earth give way and the mountains fall into the heart of the sea. . . . The LORD Almighty is with us, the God of Jacob is our fortress" (Psalm 46:1–2, 11).

God's Presence

God's presence overwhelmed me in a way I hadn't experienced before, banishing the lie of fear I'd experienced and replacing it with a confidence about the future that was unexplainable. I was filled with a peace, a calm, a supernatural assurance that could only come from the Holy Spirit. He took the written Word and made it the living Word in my heart.

Not all of my experiences of fear have been marked by similar supernatural interventions.

The lie of fear can come in many forms and in many settings.

I remember the fear that overwhelmed me as I struggled to turn around a ministry. Up until that time, every church or ministry I had touched had done a major turnaround. My formula for success was work hard, pray hard, be enthusiastic, trust God, and press ahead. . . . And everything will come out right!

Except this time it didn't. Under my watch, the ministry was sinking.

I was distraught, consumed by a gnawing sensation that I didn't have the right answers or ability. I became painfully aware of how firmly I'd attached my security and worth to my job performance. I was afraid of failure and uncertain of what would come next.

The turning point came on a vacation with my family.

Exhausted, under incredible pressure, I was coming to the realization that I was the wrong leader for the organization. As everyone else slept in, I woke up early. The only place I could find for some private time with the Lord was a walk-in closet.

In tears, I told the Lord I was sorry I'd failed and that I sensed deeply that they should find a leader who could take this ministry to the next level. Because it certainly wasn't me.

In that moment of brokenness, I heard a word from the Lord that shocked me. It was not an audible voice, but I heard it as strongly as I've ever heard anything from Him. He said, "I love you just for you, not for what you do for Me."

And then I experienced one of the most powerful emotional encounters with the Lord that I can remember. It was like I was being enveloped by His arms. I experienced being deeply loved and affirmed and valued as His son—despite my biggest ministry failure.

Years later, I sat on the couch with Theresa after learning she had cancer. All the fears I had struggled with about losing someone important to me came to the surface.

When you face a situation like that, you feel very vulnerable. All the external props that provide a sense of security, all those plans you assume you'll have time to fulfill, and all the things you think are so urgent and important seem to evaporate. In the midst of those times, you realize Jesus is your only security.

Together, Theresa and I walked through surgery and months of treatment by slowly, day by day, giving God our fears and trusting His wisdom and goodness regardless of the outcome.

Jesus promises He will be enough for you with or without your loved one, and you can cling to that truth with all your heart. You live and breathe those promises with every passing day, and His presence and peace meet you in a deeply personal way. It's in the storms of life that we get a glimpse of God and His promises move from our heads to our hearts. Each of those seasons in my life is an example of life under pressure. They are also some examples of the many ways our security gets shaken.

What Does It Mean to Be Secure?

A universal aspect of our fallen nature is deep-seated insecurity. Have you ever tried to compensate for your insecurity?

As with other aspects of our belief systems, insecurity can manifest in overcompensation or in withdrawal—in false confidence or in avoidance of threatening situations. But until we find our security in our relationship with God, it is universal. Insecurity goes down to the root of our being. Behind every mask is an insecurity about our true identity and our place in this world.

What is *security*? At a fundamental level, the noun means safety, freedom from danger or harm. People who are secure feel safe, at rest on a firm foundation.

The adjective *secure* implies certainty. It refers to a done deal. If you are secure, no outside force can come in and remove you. In a spiritual context, nothing can remove you from God.

The verb *to secure* means to obtain something without fear of losing it again.

My insecurities may be different from yours, and we may be provoked by very different fears, but all of our insecurities tend to fall into one of four categories.

In every case, security is about finding safety and certainty in an unsafe and uncertain world.

We struggle with that, don't we? I'll admit it, I'm insecure. Put me in the right circumstances, and insecurity will pop up in an instant, without fail. My insecurities may be different from yours, and we may be provoked by very different fears, but all of our insecurities tend to fall into one of four categories.

What Threatens Our Security?

These categories of insecurity are common to all of humanity and the root of many of our struggles—as well as of our unhealthy ways of responding to people and circumstances.

1. Fear of physical harm or death. Studies show that the world has never been a safer place, at least by measures relative to population size. There are fewer wars, diseases, natural disasters, and crimes per capita than there have ever been. But there's also more information about wars, diseases, disasters, and crimes than there has ever been. And paying attention to a constant stream of negative reports has magnified their effect, making us feel extremely insecure about our surroundings. Because we hear about all kinds of horrible events from every corner of the world, the threats seem very real. Many people today live in constant fear of physical harm or death.

2. *Fear of rejection or of being alone.* Insecurity convinces us of a lot of negative possibilities. *I'll never get married. If they really knew me, they wouldn't be my friends. Something is going to happen to one of my children. It's only a matter of time until my spouse gets cancer.* Many people live in constant fear of being rejected, losing a loved one, and ending up alone. Our worries make us feel alienated and vulnerable, even before we experience any of these things. If security means living without care and anxiety, few of us have found it.

3. *Fear of punishment or judgment.* I got an email recently from a young woman who had read a few Bible verses out of context and was living with the fear that she might make a mistake that would cause God to reject her forever. She was so afraid of messing up, so filled with despair, that she prayed for God to go ahead and kill her so she wouldn't risk losing her salvation. She needed reassurance that the promises of Scripture are true and that we can be secure in our relationship with God. She needed to understand how thoroughly and completely we are forgiven.

Most Christians don't wrestle with such severe anxiety, but many of us who are more aware of the reality of God's grace still live with a low-grade sense of impending judgment—a fear that every mistake puts us on God's bad side. Our theology may be completely orthodox, aligned with Scripture and the great Reformation teachers who emphasized salvation by grace through faith alone. But our experience wars against our theology in subtle ways. A lot of people have developed a language for this insecurity; we talk about how someone "must be living right" when things go well and needs to "get right with God" when they aren't. I'm amazed at how even mature believers can live with this warped sense that God is down on them and that every good or bad event is rooted in judgment. It's a disheartening, discouraging, and terrifying way to live.

4. Anxiety, guilt, doubts, and condemnation. All of these basic insecurities can produce struggles with guilt and condemnation. We feel insecure about our standing with God, then beat ourselves up for not being more secure in God's truth. We feel anxious about feeling anxious. It's a vicious cycle, with insecurity building upon insecurity while our own flaws and frailties remind us that we have every reason to doubt ourselves. When our focus turns from God's faithfulness to the weaknesses of our own faith, we lose heart. We feel as if we are constantly walking on shaky ground.

In What or Whom Do You Seek Security Apart from Christ?

The Bible says "fear not" or "do not be afraid"—or some variation thereof—well over a hundred times. Jesus's last words to His disciples assured them that He would always be with them (Matthew 28:20). God emphatically told His people that He would never leave them or forsake them (Deuteronomy 31:6; Hebrews 13:5). Still, we struggle.

That raises a very important question: If God has given us such repeated assurances, and we continue to struggle with insecurity, in what or whom are we trying to find our security? Where are we looking for it?

In this fallen world, God allows storms to come into our lives. Even if He is not the author of them, He is going to use them. He has a goal: to use them for our good and to fulfill His larger purposes.

One of the greatest biblical case studies for this is the life of Joseph. He was sold into slavery by his brothers, falsely accused by his master's wife, imprisoned for years, and then forgotten by someone who promised to mention him to the pharaoh. Again and again, he was betrayed by people who were close to him

The Bible says "fear not" or "do not be afraid"—or some variation thereof—well over a hundred times.

or who were supposed to support him. After each and every setback, the story says that "the Lord was with Joseph." In fact, his setbacks served to further God's purposes for his life, though Joseph could not have seen how at the time.

If Joseph had placed his security in the people around him, he would have given up long before God fulfilled the promises He had given him. But for thirteen long years of injustice and betrayal, he chose to put his security in the Lord, and God sustained him in every situation he faced.

As with Joseph, our journey toward the fulfillment of God's purposes for our lives rarely looks like a direct route. In fact, it can be disorienting. When we experience a few setbacks close together, we start to wonder where God is, why He has abandoned us, whether we are being disciplined or punished, or even if our desires and God's plans for us will ever be fulfilled.

We can relate to what one of the psalms says about Joseph's story: "Until the time that his word came to pass, the word of the LORD tested him" (Psalm 105:19 NASB). On the confusing path between God's promises and their fulfillment, we are tested, stretched, tried, and forged in the fires of His furnace. We go through storms, wilderness seasons, and tight spaces, and sometimes we begin to lose hope. But God's ultimate purpose is not to make us more insecure. It's to acquaint us with His ways, strengthen our faith, try our character, and ultimately to anchor our hope in God alone. Paradoxically, the things we become most insecure about are often designed to increase our sense of security.

> *Paradoxically, the things we become most insecure about are often designed to increase our sense of security.*

You probably have been through many tests, and you will go through some more. Many of them will not be especially traumatic, but occasionally you will find yourself in a crisis. In every case, you need to know and trust God's promise. He wants you to know that He will be with you, that He will never leave you or forsake you, that He is on your side. You may not believe that right now, but you will need to, and in the next chapter, we'll learn how. That is the only way you will find any real security in this world.

So, let me ask you: Where have you placed your hopes for security? Is it in *yourself*? That's been a problem for a lot of people, including me. We build our self-confidence up to mask our deeper insecurities, hoping we will never let ourselves down.

Is it in your *brains*? Some people are confident they will always be able to figure something out, even when that something is not God's solution for their problems.

Is it in *money*? Many are focused on the number of zeros in their bank account, because they reason that if there are enough of them, everything will certainly be okay.

Is it in *family*? A lot of people cannot feel secure unless their marriage, children, parents, or other family members are all doing well.

Is it in your *work*? Do you have to be in the right career, working for the right company or organization, enjoying the right benefits, and anticipating the right opportunities?

All of these relationships, possessions, and circumstances are common as objects of our misplaced desires for security.

If you want to know where you are directing your search for security, here's a test: What would devastate you if it were taken away? What challenges to your current circumstances and expectations would put you in a panic?

The answers to those questions will tell you a lot about where you have invested your hopes and what you think you need to feel secure. Your security is like a rug, and if it is pulled out from under you, it hurts. That doesn't mean that any sense of loss is an indication of misplaced security; grief is normal, and the pain of disappointment is real. But if the thought of losing something or someone provokes a fear of feeling devastated, you may be placing your security in something or someone that cannot actually make you secure. It means that you're not finding your security entirely in Christ.

The good news is that you can. Theresa and I had complete peace even if it meant she would have preceded me to heaven. I don't say that lightly or with any sense of superior spirituality. We had to learn over the years to grow and trust and put our security in Christ. Thankfully, God spared her life.

In fact, you can be eternally secure in a temporal, uncertain world. He has made provision for you and given promises to you that cannot be broken. When everything around you shakes, you can stand firm. You'll still experience pain and loss, and you'll still grieve, but you will not be devastated.

Security in Christ is unshakable. Regardless of the storms you face, you can live safely and securely in Him.

Questions for Reflection and Discussion

1) When life is shaky or tense and feels out of your control, is there someone or something you go to for security? Can true security be found in our fallen world, or is it a misconception?

2) Have you ever had a spiritual encounter with God that caused the truth of His love and promises to come alive in your heart?

3) Insecurity is common to all of humanity and is at the root of many of our lifelong struggles. Our insecurities often fall into one of these four categories:

   • Fear of physical harm or death
   • Fear of rejection or of being alone
   • Fear of punishment or judgment
   • Anxiety, guilt, doubt, and condemnation

   Which of these categories can you relate to? Why?

4) God is not the author of the storms in your life, but why does He allow them? What truths about God can you draw from Joseph's example?

5) Where have you placed your hopes for security? Is it in yourself? In money? In family? In work? If you are unsure, here's a test: What would devastate you or cause you severe panic if it were taken away?

6

You Are Secure

Ephesians 1:11–14

Believe it or not, those of us who preach for a living can often preach and teach about a subject better than actually believing it.

I'm not talking about hypocrisy here. I'm talking about passing on very important truths we're convinced we believe until we're faced with circumstances that require that we actually believe them.

In the last chapter, I shared the story of my mom's death. As a young pastor, I was faced with the reality that I could preach a very good message about heaven and eternal life, but the death of my mother presented a personal crisis: "Do you really believe that, Chip, in the depths of your soul?"

The answer resulted in an abiding sense of peace and security.

I have also fairly eloquently encouraged people not to find their identity in their work. But it's one thing to preach it and another to face a work-related failure and learn the truth about yourself.

When Theresa was diagnosed with cancer, we had no guarantees. No supernatural interventions, and no promises from God that everything would turn out right. We had to accept the fact that *God's best* might mean continued life or Theresa going home to heaven. We certainly had moments of doubt, but, throughout the entire journey, we had peace, confidence, and genuine belief because our ultimate security was in Christ.

The question is this: How exactly does that sense of peace and security happen?

What Is God's Provision for Our Security?

God offers us the kind of security that cannot be disrupted by any person or circumstance—not by the threat of cancer, natural disaster, terrorist attack, violent crime, death of a loved one, broken relationship, or anything else. We can be completely secure in Christ.

How do we know that? Peter tells us that Jesus suffered once and for all for sins—the righteous in place of the unrighteous, for the specific purpose of bringing us to God (1 Peter 3:18). His death in the flesh and resurrection by the power of the Spirit resulted in our resurrection and life with Him.

We have already seen the implications of this message: that we are *wanted, valuable, chosen, adopted, redeemed,* and *significant.* So it naturally follows that if we're treasured this much by God and restored into a relationship with Him at so high a price, that He would not hold us loosely. In fact, as we have seen, Paul wrote that nothing can separate us from Him:

> For I am convinced that neither death, nor life, nor angels, nor principalities, nor things present, nor things to come, nor powers, nor height, nor depth, nor any other created thing, will be able to separate us from the love of God, which is in Christ Jesus our Lord. (Romans 8:38–39 NASB)

This is not just an intellectual belief. Those who open up to Him by faith are given the right to become children of the living God who is sovereign over the entire universe.

I didn't know this until I was eighteen. I didn't understand very much about the gospel at the time, but I responded to the verse about Jesus standing at the door and knocking: "If anyone hears my voice and opens the door, I will come in and eat with that person, and they with me" (Revelation 3:20). Through this passage, Jesus made it clear that He wanted a relationship with me. I responded to that invitation and trusted Christ, turning from sin, asking for forgiveness, and welcoming Him as my Lord and Savior. When we make that response, the Spirit of God enters into our human body and we start a new life.

Do you understand what happens when we're saved? It isn't just an experience. It doesn't just mean we are heaven bound. It isn't just that we now know Christ. All of those things are true, but they don't capture the depth of what our salvation means. They don't describe the complete transformation that takes place within us.

Life as a New Creation

What actually happens when we receive Christ is enough to undo all of our insecurities. Our understanding affects the way we think and feel; our thoughts and feelings prompt our actions; and our actions shape our lives. So, knowing the truth about our salvation—that it addresses the root of our fears and anxieties—has everything to do with how we experience God and live securely.

THINKING > EMOTIONS > BEHAVIOR > CONSEQUENCES

What we think about God determines whether we will look for our security in sex and intimacy, addictions and habits, money and possessions, accomplishments and jobs, and every other avenue the mind might take to find peace. If we don't understand who God is and what He has done, we begin to look for security in all the wrong places, and pain is multiplied in our lives. God wants us to avoid all of that frustration and futility.

The theological terms that describe our salvation include *justification*, *regeneration*, *reconciliation*, *propitiation*, and *sanctification*. If you want to dig into those terms some more, I've included descriptions of each at the end of this chapter. But the main thing to understand is that when you receive Christ by faith, you become an entirely new person in God's sight. And as you learn to see through God's eyes, you begin to see yourself in entirely new ways.

First of all, you can rest in the fact that all of your sins—past, present, and future—are forgiven. You are legally declared righteous. Imagine, for example, that your picture and name have come up on the screen of God's computer. Under your name are all the things you've ever thought, said, or done that were less than perfect, with less-than-perfect motives. Now imagine that Jesus's name pops up on the other side of the screen, and under His name are all His righteous deeds and perfect character.

Your Name	Jesus
Your Sins	His Righteousness
• Past	• _____
• Present	• _____
• Future	• _____

When you're saved, God clicks Delete and removes all your sins from your record. Then, with His supernatural cursor, He selects all of Jesus's righteousness and pastes it to your page. Not only are your sins removed, but you now possess the righteousness of Christ.

We, therefore, have peace with God. According to Scripture, we were once hostile to God and opposed to His purposes for our lives. He brings the kind of peace that ends that hostility and makes us His allies. We are not only at peace with Him; we are now in His family. You are His holy, beloved, treasured, and adored child. And what do good fathers do for their beloved children? They watch over them with great care. They protect and provide. They make sure their children are safe and secure.

As a new creation in Christ, you become a new person. "The old things passed away; behold, new things have come" (2 Corinthians 5:17 NASB). The common illustration for this metamorphosis is one we learned in basic biology. A caterpillar creates a chrysalis, and out comes a butterfly. The little green caterpillar and the bright, beautiful butterfly have exactly the same DNA, but a fundamental transformation has taken place. The caterpillar has taken on a new nature. It has new capabilities. It is no longer small and ugly; it is beautiful and new.

You are His holy, beloved, treasured, and adored child.

As someone who has been spiritually reborn (John 3:1–7), you will need to learn to think as a new creation. You may need to remind yourself often of who you are, to retrain your thoughts to adhere to truth. Far too many Christians are living under the weight of their past: all the things they have been through, all the people who have let them down, all the dysfunction in their families of origin or their adult relationships, all the addictions and habits and sins that keep them captive. And while it's true that our past actions still carry future consequences, there is a fundamental break with our past when we personally receive Christ. A profound change has taken place. We no longer have to crawl. We can fly.

Christians who are still crawling don't understand their new nature; they haven't stepped into it yet. That's a process for all of us, and none of us are walking in our new nature as fully as we could. But we need to realize the power that is available to us. We are new people because the risen

Jesus lives in us. We live from another realm and carry a new nature.

Even though we were once hostile to God and alienated from Him, He has so thoroughly cleansed us and redeemed us that when we believe in Jesus, we are now guilt free and reconciled with Him (Colossians 1:21–22). We're on His side, and He is on ours. Knowing Him is infinitely more worthwhile than knowing any influential athlete, performer, or political leader. We have the invaluable privilege of being His friends.

Unfortunately, I meet many Christians who don't see God as a friend. They see Him as an unrelenting evaluator who is down on them and never pleased with who they are or how they live. I think that coming to believe God is my friend has done as much as anything to transform my relationship with Him. Friends hang out together, enjoy each other's company, and are available in times of need. They share life together without jealousy or division. They walk through the good times and the bad together. They don't judge each other, but they do challenge each other when things need to change. They develop a lifelong bond.

That's what our reconciliation with God does for us. As we learn to believe that God is our friend, we stop feeling responsible to do the right thing in order to get right with Him. By faith, we are already right with God. We no longer think, *I need to pray longer, I need to read the Bible more, I need to give more, I need to do the right things so God will be okay with me.* Instead, we begin to think about ways to enjoy His company, to grow closer to Him, to hear His voice in Scripture, to experience His presence and receive His wisdom and counsel, and to walk in His ways. That's why Jesus told some religious people, "Come to me, all you who are weary and burdened, and I will give you rest" (Matthew 11:28). He wants to help us through this life, not by laying more burdens on our shoulders but by taking them off so we can simply live with Him.

God didn't lose His righteous anger when He forgave our sins. He redirected it. When Jesus was hanging on the cross and crying out, "My God, my God, why have you forsaken me?" the wrath of God for all of the sins human beings have committed, large and small, was being poured onto this innocent, righteous man and diverted away from us. God took the punishment each of us deserves and placed it on Christ. In that moment, the Father turned away from the sin bearer and let our guilt fall on Him. He lifted the weight of our sin once and for all.

What does that mean for our security? For one thing, it means that God will never punish those who are in Christ. That would be redundant. He would not pour out His wrath on Jesus at the cross and then turn around and pour out His wrath on those who believe in Jesus as the sacrifice for their sins. It also means we don't have to be afraid to die. There was a time when I was deeply fearful at the thought of death, but no more. We are secure in Jesus for all eternity.

You may have all kinds of objections rising up in the back of your mind about all the things you've done. But whatever happened in your past, you still need to understand that all the punishment you deserved is fully satisfied in the work of

Christ. God may discipline you from time to time as a loving means of guiding you back into His will when you've strayed from it—I call it the velvet vise of grace that He uses to get our attention (see Hebrews 12:4–11)—but your punishment has been dealt with forever.

Far too many people, even Christians, live with the assumption that God is angry and displeased with them. But if you have received Jesus, judgment has already been rendered in your case. Your salvation has already been accomplished.

Let me say this emphatically: *God is not mad at you.* He knew about your sins before you were born, and He chose you and adopted you anyway. The sacrifice of Jesus had already been planned before the foundation of the world. God has already placed His anger on Christ for a moment so we could be free from His anger for eternity. Our sins make Him sad—they are essentially a rejection of His good and kind will for us—and He will guide us away from them, firmly when necessary. But we no longer need to be afraid of His punishment.

When I began to grasp that my sinful choices and actions didn't make God mad but made Him sad, it changed how I lived. Sin isn't simply doing wrong or crossing a line; it's personal. It hurts my Father after all He's done for me. Since the punishment for my sin is already covered, it changes how I approach everything.

It is often said that God accepts us the way we are but will not leave us that way, and it's true. He'll never leave us alone. He's teaching us how to live as a new creation as His sons and daughters. The Spirit of God dwells inside of us, enabling

105

us to allow Christ to live His life through us by His power. Much of that is our responsibility, but the power comes from Him. We are being transformed through a joint venture between the Holy Spirit and our own willingness to cooperate with Him.

Transformation is a process, and you will find that your relationship with the Lord is determined by your relationship with His Word.

> *Your relationship with the Lord is determined by your relationship with His Word.*

Your relationship with God is also determined by your relationship with the rest of His body. No one can live the Christian life alone. You can't say no to malice and envy and the rest of your old nature without the encouragement and support of other believers. You will need advice and counsel. You will need others to spur you on when you aren't able to keep going by yourself. That's part of how God designed us. We're wired to be interdependent. Doing life in community with other believers and being rooted in God's Word are prerequisites to experiencing the fullness of this salvation that makes us secure.

Can you imagine what would happen if you embraced everything your salvation says about you and made some significant psychological shifts? How would it feel to go from "God feels distant" to "God is my Father"? Or from "I'm a prisoner of my past" to "I'm a new person"? Or from "I need to earn God's favor" to "I am God's friend"? Can you imagine what it would be like to never fear God's judgment again—to never question in the midst of a crisis if the reason behind it is God's punishment for something you did?

I can promise you that making these shifts will have a dramatic effect on the way you live. Embracing these truths will completely reorient your perspective on life and its challenges. The fullness of your salvation gives you everything you need to be completely secure in an insecure world.

Can We Know for Certain We Are Secure?

There is no absolute security in this fallen world. You've lived through enough experiences, seen enough headlines, and suffered enough losses to understand the transient and temporal nature of life. Each of us is one earthquake, tsunami, car wreck, stock market crash, or doctor's report away from a significant life change. Nothing you believe about God or yourself is going to eliminate those possibilities. What you can do is change where you look for your security—away from things that cannot guarantee it and toward the God who has given you multiple assurances that you're safe in Him forever.

When you prayed to receive Christ, God became your Father and Friend, and you became a new person. He promises He will never punish you or leave you.

But how can we know and experience this supernatural security that we already possess? The answer is found in Ephesians 1. It tells us we can know for certain that we are secure:

> *In Him* also we have obtained an inheritance, having been predestined according to His purpose who works all things

after the counsel of His will, to the end that we who were the first to hope in Christ would be to the praise of His glory. *In Him*, you also, after listening to the message of truth, the gospel of your salvation—having also believed, you were sealed in Him with the Holy Spirit of promise, *who is given as a pledge of our inheritance*, with a view to the redemption of God's own possession, to the praise of His glory. (Ephesians 1:10–14 NASB)

When Paul writes "we" in this context, he is referring to Jews. *We Jews*, who were the first to hope in Christ, were chosen as the vehicle for God's purposes according to His deliberate, strategic choice ("the purpose of his will"). This is not any impersonal, passive, reluctant expression of God's will. It springs from a warm, deep emotion. Paul is essentially saying, "We Jews were enthusiastically chosen by God to be agents of His blessing."

But in the middle of this passage, Paul turns to "you," the Gentiles who are reading this letter. "And you also were included in Christ" (v. 13). Gentiles heard the message and believed, which resulted in their salvation. And then Paul makes a remarkable statement that guarantees our security in this salvation: we were sealed with the Holy Spirit of promise. There is no greater guarantee than that.

In Roman culture, this seal refers to a sale. It's like a title deed, a written statement that the transaction is complete. It can't be taken back. It finalizes ownership and makes it secure. So when we believed in Christ, every aspect of our salvation occurred or began to occur. In addition, we were sealed with the Spirit of God—and not just the Spirit, but the "Spirit of promise." When God makes a promise, it is irrevocable. Some of His promises may be conditional, but, in this case, the condition (faith) has already been met. If we truly repented and trusted Christ, we have an irrevocable salvation.

In fact, it gets even better. The Holy Spirit is given to us as a "deposit"—or "pledge" (NASB)—of our inheritance. The picture here is of a down payment or of earnest money. Just as we put down a payment on a car or house to seal the deal and begin using it, God has put down His Spirit into our hearts as a guarantee of what is to come.

He is saying, "I want you to know that I've sealed you for Myself, and this measure of My Spirit is evidence that one day I am going to pull everything together for the fullness of your redemption and inheritance. Your true self will be fully mature, you will have a new body, your freedom will be complete, and you will share in everything Jesus inherits. You will live in a new heaven and a new earth, and you will be with Me forever and ever." That's security, and it won't ever change.

That's why God never wants us to live with fear and anxiety. We are His children, co-heirs with Jesus, assured of an eternal inheritance, and sealed with His Spirit as a down payment. In other words, you and I are unfathomably rich and secure.

Is that how you see yourself? Have you ever fully grasped the absolute certainty of your future—both now and forever? If not, let me help you take your next steps to experiencing security in Christ.

How to See Yourself as God Sees You

As always, the process of change begins with replacing lies with truth. If you've been making index cards from the lies and truths discussed in earlier chapters, you may have already begun to notice a change in your attitude. Even if those changes are very subtle, keep at it. If the son of an alcoholic can marry the rejected daughter of an alcoholic, go through painfully difficult learning experiences and mistakes, and still come through with solid faith and hope in God and numerous testimonies of His goodness like Theresa and I have, then you can experience radical change too. Misbeliefs eventually give way to truth, and God is faithful to transform us. What we must remember is that we are the product of our thought life, and we're in a very real battle with the father of lies.

One of the fundamental lies that undermines our security is this: *those who fail are unworthy of love and deserve to be punished*. I believed that lie for a long time, and it drove me to try to earn love, prove myself, and perform perfectly. For others, this lie causes them to avoid failure by withdrawing and never putting themselves on the line. Neither response enables us to receive the love of God and live in the security He promises.

Below, I've written those two misbeliefs on a card like the one Theresa and I reviewed daily for two years. After reading those lies out loud, we would say, "STOP!" and then turn the card over and read the "Security Truth" and Bible passage. Take a moment to read the truth on the card in the diagram.

We are secure because we have been sealed by the Spirit. If you have received Christ by faith, everything written on

Misbelief

- Those who fail are unworthy of love and deserve to be punished.

- Doubt, guilt over past mistakes, and condemnation are evidence that I am a bad person and unworthy of being loved by God or others.

Truth

I am secure in my relationship with Christ, in my daily safety and well-being, and in my future outlook, whether on earth or in heaven, because I have been sealed by the Holy Spirit.

"Surely goodness and lovingkindness will follow me all the days of my life, and I will dwell in the house of the Lord forever."
Psalm 23:6 (NASB)

that "Security Truth" card is true for you as well. Isn't that awesome?

As we close this chapter, if you realize you are still outside of Christ—that you have never owned up to the fact that you have sinned against a holy God, never turned away from self and sin and asked Him to forgive you and come into your life. I invite you to do that right now. There is nothing stopping you. You have a loving Father who has made all of these amazing, precious promises and privileges to gain, and you have nothing to lose but futility and frustration.

If you sense God prompting you to respond to Him, tell Him something like this: "Lord, I want what you've offered in Christ. I want to know You and receive Your Spirit and the fullness of salvation. I want to be Your child. I want to enter into the eternal inheritance You have promised. I ask You to forgive me on the basis of Jesus's work on the cross and His resurrection. I believe Jesus died in my place and paid for my sins. I ask You right now to come into my life and raise me to new life in Him. Amen."

Now transfer your trust from all the things of the world and place it in Him alone. If you've done that in truth and sincerity, you're secure. You're anchored in His love, a citizen of heaven, and safe in His arms for all of eternity.

If you just prayed to receive Christ and have become a member of His family, make sure you tell someone today. Also, I'd love to help you get started in your new life. Visit living ontheedge.org/new-believers to download a free digital resource to help you on your journey.

Questions for Reflection and Discussion

1) How does your thinking affect your actions? Think of an example.

2) Read Romans 8:38–39 (NASB):

> For I am convinced that neither death, nor life, nor angels, nor principalities, nor things present, nor things to come, nor powers, nor height, not depth, nor any other created thing, will be able to separate us from the love of God, which is in Christ Jesus our Lord.

What truths about the love of God stand out to you in this passage?

3) What is the difference between living to "get right with God" versus living as someone who "is already right with Him"?

4) Does God punish those who are in Christ? Why not? How do Jesus's words on the cross, "My God, my God, why have you forsaken me?" confirm that there is no condemnation for those in Jesus?

5) If you truly believe that your sinful choices and actions don't make God mad but make Him sad, how does that change the way you approach your life and your relationship with God?

6) Pick one of the truths from below to write out and place somewhere you can read it every day. Ask God

for His help in moving this truth from your head to your heart and living in its freedom.

Truths:

- God gave me a new nature. Old things have passed away. I am a new person. I don't have to live with my past anymore, even if people remind me of it. God sees me as new.
- God is my friend. He is my Father. He has made me holy and blameless. I am no longer hostile to Him or His ways. I no longer live in guilt and shame. I am new, free, and whole.

What Actually Happens When We Receive Christ?

Our security is rooted in our salvation, so when we receive Christ by faith, we're completely secure in Him. It's one thing to have security, however, and another to experience it. Only when we begin to understand what God actually accomplished for us in Christ do we begin to feel secure.

We receive all of these blessings the moment we receive Christ, though some of them will need to work their way into our lives over time. When we accept Christ by faith,

We are justified. All our sins are forgiven and we're given the righteousness of Jesus. It's a legal decision that applies to all our sins, whether past, present, or future. It's what Paul was getting at in that unfathomable statement that God made Jesus to become sin on our behalf so that we might become the righteousness of God in Him (2 Corinthians 5:21). God's verdict is that we have a clean slate. Our sins went with Jesus into the grave, and His righteousness is given to us instead.

We are no longer under God's judgment but are free to live as His dearly loved children.

The implications of our justification, according to Scripture, are that we can consider ourselves dead to sin but alive to God (Romans 6:11), that it is no longer we who live but Christ who lives in us (Galatians 2:20), that there is no condemnation for those who are in Christ (Romans 8:1), and that we have peace with God (Romans 5:1).

We are regenerated. When a rabbi named Nicodemus—a Pharisee, a member of the ruling council, a moral role model, and a man with his reputation at stake—came to Jesus secretly at night, Jesus gave him some life-changing advice: "No one can see the kingdom of God unless they are born again" (John 3:3). If we want to enter the kingdom of God, we have to be reborn spiritually.

That's what regeneration means. It's a new birth. Jesus taught a religious, moral man—a pillar of Jewish society— that spiritual birth is the only way into God's kingdom. You cannot see the ways of God unless you receive a new nature.

"If anyone is in Christ, he is a new creature; the old things passed away; behold, new things have come" (2 Corinthians 5:17 NASB). The verb tenses in the original language of this verse are fascinating. The old is past tense; it has already passed away at the point we receive Christ by faith. The new is present progressive; all things are in the process of becoming new. The new creation is already a reality, but we're growing in our experience of it. Just as a caterpillar has the full DNA of a butterfly within it but must grow into its new appearance, God is in the process of growing us and restoring our lives.

We are reconciled. Even though we were once hostile to God and alienated from Him, we are now His friends. "Once you were alienated from God and were enemies in your minds because of your evil behavior, but now he has reconciled you by Christ's physical body through death to present you holy in his sight, without blemish and free from accusation" (Colossians

1:21–22). As we digest this truth, absorb it, and believe it more deeply, it begins to change us. It becomes part of our focus in life and shapes how we see God, ourselves, and the world around us. Not many Christians have fully embraced what this passage says about them: that we're "holy in his sight, without blemish and free from accusation." But it's true. That's how God sees us in Christ.

Because we're reconciled with God, we no longer need to try to get right with Him. We *are* right with Him, and we can celebrate that fact and rest in it. We are friends with the God of the universe.

We receive propitiation for our sins. We hardly ever hear the word "propitiation" today in normal conversation, so not many people know how to define it. It means that Jesus satisfied the wrath of God by His death on the cross when He took all our punishment on Himself. This transaction doesn't need to be renewed; it's a once-for-all, forever-and-ever event: "By this the love of God was manifested in us, that God has sent His only begotten Son into the world so that we might live through Him. In this is love, not that we loved God, but that He loved us and sent His Son to be the propitiation for our sins. Beloved, if God so loved us, we also ought to love one another" (1 John 4:9–11 NASB).

God is opposed to evil and has righteous anger toward everything that contradicts His love. All sorts of injustices have been committed in the name of greed, ego, power trips, and selfish ambition. These things anger God because they are an affront to everything that is just and good and godly. But when Jesus was hanging on the cross and crying out, "My God, my God, why have you forsaken me?" the wrath of God for all these sins, large and small, was being poured onto this innocent, righteous man and diverted away from us. God took the punishment each of us deserves and placed it on Christ. In that moment, the Father turned away from the sin bearer and let our guilt fall on Him. He lifted the weight of our sin once and for all. The bottom line is that no matter what you've done, He is not mad at you.

We are sanctified. Sanctification means we're cleansed of our sin, set apart to God, and growing in righteousness. To be clear, we're declared holy immediately—the New Testament always refers to Christians as saints, not sinners—but we only experience sanctification over time. It is a journey in which the Holy Spirit transforms our inner attitudes and outward actions to come into alignment with the image of Christ. Where justification is primarily about our legal position in God's eyes, the emphasis in sanctification is practical righteousness—how we live it out day by day. As we walk by faith and obedience, trust in God's promises, and give and receive encouragement in the body of Christ, we grow in our experience of grace. God, through the Holy Spirit living within us, progressively transforms us into the likeness of Jesus.

Peter describes this process: "Rid yourselves of all malice and all deceit, hypocrisy, envy, and slander of every kind. Like newborn babies, crave pure spiritual milk, so that by it you may grow up in your salvation" (1 Peter 2:1–2). The first sentence is all about leaving the old nature behind; the second is all about embracing the new nature and growing up in it.

In some of his letters, Paul describes this process in terms of taking off old clothes and putting on new ones. We may have a new nature, but the Bible is clear that the flesh and spirit wage war against each other, and we choose which side will actually win in our daily experience.

So, Peter places these instructions in the context of all that God has done for us. Sanctification is one of the major themes of his first letter, from the opening verses. So, on one hand, we're told that we are already holy (Colossians 3:12); on the other, we're told to be holy (1 Peter 1:15–16). The first is how God already sees us; the second is how we are to live out our new nature. We set aside the things of our past and embrace our true selves.

If you fully embrace these truths and live in awareness of what God has done for you through salvation, your life will be changed. It will reorient your perspective. The fullness of your salvation gives you everything you need to be completely secure in an insecure world.

PART 4

COMPETENT

7

The Lie of Shame

My wife lived with tremendous shame. In her first marriage, she was abandoned by an unbelieving husband who ran off with another woman and left her with two small babies. Theresa's boss cared for her enough to share the gospel with her. He told her every day at work that Jesus loved her and would help her.

After about a year of hearing that day after day, Theresa went to a little church where her boss was the lay preacher, and during the service, she felt nothing. Her heart sank because she desperately wanted to find God if He existed. As hope was seeping out of her soul, she made her way to the parking lot. As she was walking out, an eighty-five-year-old woman named Mrs. McGrady saw her open the door and put her two children into the car and said, "Hey, young lady, do you want to be saved?"

"Yes," Theresa said.

"Then let's go back into that church and ask God to come into your life." Theresa did, and the whole congregation joined her as she knelt at the altar. In that moment, God revealed Himself to her in a powerful way. Mrs. McGrady didn't know Theresa at all, but she listened to that still, small voice and was confident and bold. The result was that Theresa met and accepted Christ.

Theresa didn't feel shame at that church, but she did when I was in seminary. After learning Theresa had been divorced, another student said, "I didn't know they let people like you in here." So in our first church ministry, she didn't tell anyone about her background. She didn't want to subject herself to those shaming attitudes again. She felt like a second-class citizen.

When those two babies, my older boys, were about four years old, they were in our wedding—and, naturally, in our wedding pictures. So, when our third son, Ryan, got old enough to ask those honest and awkward questions kids have a knack for asking, he said, "Hey, Mommy, how come I didn't get to be in the wedding like Eric and Jason?" That question made Theresa realize how much shame she still felt—so much that she had never told our own son about our family background.

Thank God for Bill Lawrence, whose story I told in chapter 1. While we were at seminary, he helped Theresa understand that no matter how much people and even the church might shame her, God doesn't. She was, and would always be, His precious daughter. Bill told her, "You are a trophy of God's grace." His words were a turning point in her life.

As evidence of how much Theresa was freed from her shame, one of the first things she did when we began our second church ministry years ago at Santa Cruz Bible Church was to give her testimony. It was the Sunday evening service of our first weekend there. It was a big, bold step, and she was very nervous, but it changed the course of her life as well as the lives of countless other women.

When she finished speaking, more than fifty women stood waiting to talk to her. It's like God opened a valve of hope through her story and let them know that they also could be trophies of God's grace. Theresa's vulnerability and courage in that moment was powerfully healing for her, and it launched her ministry with women that continues to this day.

The long and challenging journey of reviewing the Affirmation Cards (see chap. 1) in the mornings and consistently saying out loud who she was in Christ had allowed her to break free of the prison of shame. Now I had the joy of watching my wife, after she had gone public with her background, live with a new joy and freedom in Christ. Theresa later led a women's retreat for our church that she entitled Precious in His Sight, and the response was tremendous. Years later, something unusual happened. As I was reading emails from many of our Living on the Edge listeners, many of them women, I got the idea of putting one of Theresa's messages on the air, along with the Affirmation Cards.

The response was stunning. Women responded to her teaching en masse. It was so amazing that our chief operating officer said, "Chip, I don't want to make you feel bad, but we've never had such a quick and overwhelming response to a message and resources like this."

God turned the pain of Theresa's past into a healing balm for thousands of women across America. Her shame became God's fame, and people have found hope and love through her story—not because she has it all together but because she was willing to say, "Yes, this is part of my past. Some of the mistakes were mine. Some were what other people did to me. But I am a daughter of the King. God is my Father, and I am redeemed, adopted, loved, and secure."

She knows her true identity, and she no longer has any need for secrets or pretense.

The Debilitating Power of Shame

Shame rarely shows up on the surface. It's one of those hidden secrets in our soul, something we carry behind our masks, an unhealed spiritual and emotional wound that seems to scar us for life. Every day, you will talk with people, sit in the same room with them, and pass them on the street without any awareness of the shame they're carrying. On the outside, they may seem to have it all together, but deep down, they're suffering from the relentless feeling that something is seriously wrong with them—that if people only knew, they would keep their distance.

Shame disguises itself as your true self, but it isn't. It feels like it's rooted in who you are but is usually only rooted in something you've done or that's been done to you. It may come from a broken relationship, a secret affair, a hidden abortion, an addiction, a promiscuous past, or anything else that makes you feel like a second-class Christian—or even a second-class person.

Sometimes the shame doesn't come from anything you did but from what someone else did to you—from a stolen innocence, a violated trust, an abuse of your deepest self. It doesn't matter how long ago it was; if the wound has never healed, it can feel very much in the present, and it will continue to fester. Even if you're walking with God now, shame can well up with an embarrassing memory, a phone call, a song on the radio, or a reconnection with someone you used to know.

> *Shame disguises itself as your true self, but it isn't.*

Whenever it bubbles to the surface, it makes you feel like part of you is unlovable and you're being punished. It masquerades as unpardonable sin.

You can often tell how strong your sense of shame is by how zealously you hide your past from friends and family members. The last thing you want is for people to know what you used to be like. It feels like part of your identity must remain forever hidden. Shame drives you to cover your true self, compensate for your past, or withdraw from any risk of exposing it.

It's both sad and fascinating to spend time with a group of people who look like everything is going well in their lives only to discover the turmoil they have been carrying beneath the surface for years. My wife has spent a lot of time with various groups of bright, competent, successful women, and it's always surprising when she tells me about the pain they're dealing with. She never tells me any names or details, but she often says, "Chip, you would not believe the amount of pain in our church."

She has told me discreetly and anonymously of people who have spent decades grieving a parent's suicide, who carry the scars of sexual abuse, of relatives in prison, and so much more. It's enough to convince me that most people have long wrestled with deep shame in some area of their lives.

We began this book with the theological thesis that the most important thing about us is how we see God, and the second most important thing about us is what comes to mind when we think about ourselves—the mirror in our minds.

If that's true, and I strongly believe it is, then shame is an enemy that has some of the most distorting effects on our identities. Among all the fears and feelings that warp our perspectives, shame is perhaps the most devastating.

What Exactly Is Shame?

Shame is a painful feeling of regret, self-hatred, and dishonor. Brené Brown describes it as the "painful feeling or experience of believing we are flawed and therefore unworthy of love and belonging."[1] I've heard it said that a person who's struggling with guilt says, "I did something bad," but a person who's struggling with shame says, "I *am* bad." It's an attack not on behavior but on identity.

126

Whatever shame looks like, it's debilitating. It marks your life. It keeps you from believing you are worthy. And if you've ever been convinced of your shame, you know that any talk of God as a loving Father, any promise of salvation as a comprehensive solution to our deepest needs, or even any compliment for a job well done comes across like BBs bouncing off of a tank.

A person who's struggling with guilt says, "I did something bad," but a person who's struggling with shame says, "I am bad."

Truths coming in from the outside hardly penetrate deeply felt shame. A person steeped in shame will continue to feel the need to perform and behave to make themselves feel worthy of love and acceptance.

When I preach about this, I can see the expressions and body language of virtually every member of our congregation responding with sadness and despair while trying desperately to hide those reactions. What is encouraging about my observation is that it involves so many people. Every person who thinks they are fighting this battle alone is actually a member of a very large club. If you've struggled with shame, you need to know you're not alone. You aren't in the minority. You're experiencing a universal phenomenon.

Perhaps the only redeeming aspect of shame is that even though it (shame) usually results in guilt and self-deprecation, shame can also lead us to God and His answers. It sends us in search of a Savior. As natural as shame can feel, however much it seems to become part of our identity, it's not a reflection of our true selves. Deep down, something inside us knows that.

When we encounter the gospel and its promise to address our shame, our spirit responds. We're drawn to freedom. We instinctively know we need someone to rescue us from this debilitating force.

And in Jesus, we find a powerful antidote to our deepest, most personal wounds.

Unhealthy Responses to Shame

Tragically, unresolved shame creates quite a few unhealthy dynamics in our lives, even when we're not fully conscious of them. Shame produces feelings of inferiority, which can affect our relationships, undermine our confidence, and limit our willingness to engage in social activities or make commitments. This sense of inferiority may never be visible to others, and sometimes we may not even be aware of it ourselves. But it creates certain assumptions when we interact with the world around us, and those assumptions can allow others to take advantage of us or manipulate us.

Even though shame usually results in guilt and self-deprecation, it can also lead us to God and His answers.

The fears and feelings of inferiority attached to shame can also prompt self-destructive behaviors—private lives marked by duplicity, addictions, pornography, substance abuse, self-medication, and many other bad decisions. Some of these may make us feel more powerful or confident in the moment, but they have adverse effects down the road. Lust and pornography, for example, make a guy feel manlier in the short run and much less manly later. An affair begins with the thrill of the forbidden and ends with guilt and destroyed relationships. The rush of shopping for new things can put us in deeper debt next month. Our attempts at covering up or overcompensating almost always come with regret. They perpetuate the cycle by producing more shame, adding to the feeling that if people really knew your true self, they would reject you.

> *The fears and feelings of inferiority attached to shame can also prompt self-destructive behaviors.*

Shame can also result in self-pity or despair. I often hear about suicides of people who were doing well but lost their job or their marriage and couldn't face the future. For some, shame leads to passivity or withdrawal due to a fear of taking risks, of putting themselves in a vulnerable position, of using their gifts and talents because of the criticism that might follow, or of being proactive about potential problems.

Shame can lead us in the other direction too, producing compulsiveness, drivenness, and overcompensation. I covered my shame by being the overachiever. I felt the shame of being the shortest kid in my class. I believed I never measured up to my dad's expectations. The message I heard was that I couldn't make it. As a result, I lived most of my early life apart from Christ with the attitude, "I'll show you! You'll see what someone short and skinny can do if he works harder and longer than everyone else." That imprint is a lie and has taken me years to understand and overcome. I've had to renew my mind to think, *I don't need to prove anything to anyone. I am loved and accepted by my heavenly Father.*

Some feel pain and shame every time they look in the mirror. They don't like how they look and are extremely self-conscious about it. Young women in our society are often overwhelmed with the ideals of being skinny enough, beautiful enough, and smart enough to impress—and if they aren't, they don't measure up.

The message is harsh and unrelenting: there's something wrong with you. In terms of grades, degrees, careers, and income, girls have never been more successful than they are now, but they have never felt more inadequate. Teen depression and suicide are off the charts.[2] Society does its share in creating that shame, but parents often contribute to it unwittingly by emphasizing how important it is to excel and strive for the next level, no matter how much their children have already accomplished. These demands often come from good intentions, but they create young people who feel ashamed that they never measure up. The results can be devastating.

Where I live in the Silicon Valley, the pressure to have perfect grades and high test scores and to get into the Stanfords and Harvards of the world is suffocating. Each year multiple students commit suicide when they achieve less than the ideal. In their minds, they are worthless, have not measured up, and have brought shame to their families.

Shame can lead to all kinds of self-destructive behaviors like isolation or cutting, or self-soothing behaviors like abusing substances, being an adrenaline junkie, and hooking up with friends who are bad influences. Some seek out sedatives and stimulants to deaden the pain or cover it. I've known people who felt the urge to move to another city every three or four years just to disconnect from problems and disappointing relationships and start over; others who go shopping every time they need a rush and end up under mountains of debt; and still others who get married or have a child just to revamp their image and feel better about themselves.

All of these things can be setups for failure, lead to even greater problems, and ultimately result in significantly more shame. Even when success is achieved, it's never enough. The wounds of shame are never healed with quick, superficial efforts.

Unhealthy Responses to Shame

- inferiority
- destructive behaviors
- self-pity
- passivity
- withdrawal/hiding
- drivenness
- codependency
- self-loathing
- a distorted body image

How Have You Dealt with Shame Apart from Christ?

So, how do you deal with your shame? Despite how you may feel after reading the last few paragraphs, I'm not trying to be negative or discouraging. I'm seeking to help you realize how pervasive, powerful, and destructive shame can be in our lives. The good news is coming soon, but facing the truth always precedes being healed by the truth.

In all likelihood, some of these descriptions have resonated with you. As painful as it can be to bring these things to the surface, let me encourage you to do a little self-analysis. In what ways are you most tempted to deal with shame? Do you depend on any particular habits or behaviors to find relief from your pain? Has shame or a sense of inferiority produced dysfunctional relationship patterns? Are you living in fear that someone might find out about the secrets of your past? Do you struggle with self-hatred, self-pity, or self-image issues? Do you have tendencies toward compulsive behavior, or do you withdraw from potentially embarrassing or shaming situations? Do you sedate or stimulate to cover your pain?

Facing the truth always precedes being healed by the truth.

Please don't push these questions away. They may make you feel very uncomfortable, but your heavenly Father wants to help you, and that begins with honesty. You have nothing to be ashamed about that is not common to the human condition. You're not a freak or an oddball.

You came into this world as a fallen human being, and part of that fallenness is getting caught in a cycle of shame that only God can heal. But in order for Him to heal your shame, you'll need to bring it to the surface. Identify it, call it out, and take it to Him. As we'll see in the next chapter, He has amazing healing powers and the perfect antidote to all our shame.

======= **Questions for Reflection and Discussion** =======

1) How is shame like an emotional wound or a scar?

2) Shame can disguise itself as the real you and may feel like it is rooted in who you are, but it is usually rooted in something that you have done or that has been done to you. Do you agree? Why or why not?

3) Shame is perhaps the strongest enemy of our identity, distorting it and profoundly damaging it. Shame says, "You are bad, unworthy of love, and all alone." How has shame distorted your identity?

4) Unhealthy responses to shame may include inferiority, destructive behaviors, self-pity, passivity, withdrawal, drivenness, codependency, self-loathing, or a distorted body image. Do you see any of these responses in your life? If so, which ones?

5) Your loving, heavenly Father wants to heal you, and He *can* heal you. But healing begins with honesty—honesty with yourself to identify your shame, call it out, and take it to Him. What shame are you carrying? Take it to God.

6) There is healing, joy, and hope in telling others your testimony. Although you may be nervous and unsure, tell your story to a friend this week. Tell your friend what God has done in your life.

8

You Are Competent

Ephesians 1:15–23

The auditorium was packed, electric with energy and anticipation. When the speaker, a woman named Valerie, stepped onto the platform and began to share, my jaw dropped.

I was stunned at Valerie's ability to communicate, at how her ministry to women with unwanted pregnancies started, at the high-tech medical equipment they used, at the hundreds of women who had been helped, and at the multitude of babies who had been saved in the last twelve months. In all my years, I had never witnessed the level of excellence, passion, and impact that Valerie and her team had accomplished.

In about fifteen minutes, I would make my way to the platform to speak, yet I found myself so enthralled with what Valerie was saying that I almost forgot why I was there.

Minutes later, I stepped onto the platform with a renewed energy and urgency to inspire others in the room to join Valerie on her mission to rescue unborn children, and to educate young women about why our Creator values every human life—especially those in the womb who have no voice.

Valerie's passion and conviction were contagious, and I wondered what made her such a powerful communicator. Before I finished speaking, I was prompted by the Holy Spirit to donate my honorarium to help the cause, and I learned afterward that my wife, who attended with me, also felt compelled to give. I went to inspire others and left thrilled to get to participate in what God was doing through Valerie and her team.

My curiosity was ignited. What was it about Valerie that made her so compelling, and how could she start and grow a ministry with such impact? Her ministry, Real Options, has multiple locations and continues to flourish in the heart of one of the most progressive cities in America. I had to find out why.

Shortly after the event, I called Valerie to catch up with her, hear how things went, and explore the *why* behind what I saw and heard at the event.

Valerie had an abortion and kept it a secret for years. Eventually, she realized it could not remain a secret. The abortion was a mistake, but she knew she was forgiven and released the shame she'd felt. Then she recruited a team to help the many women who have had similar experiences. Today, the lives of thousands of women are different because of how Valerie and her team have helped them find love and healing. Thousands of babies are alive because Valerie let go of her shame and decided to help others make the right decision.

Valerie determined to let God's forgiveness, not her shame, define her. She embraced her true identity: "I am His daughter, and He wants to turn my shame into His fame," she says. "He has made me a trophy on his mantel. He has given me hope, so I can give hope to others."

What Is God's Antidote for Shame?

Shame is powerful and debilitating, but it is not as powerful as grace. God has had a solution for it even from the beginning. The first time we see it in Scripture is in Eden, where Adam and Eve tried to hide themselves from God after they sinned. Their shame was understandable. They knew the right thing to do, had the ability and the nature to make the right choice, and chose to defy God anyway. So they hid from God, covered themselves with fig leaves, and tried to ignore the problem.

God dealt with shame then the same way He does now. He asked a question to induce an honest answer: "Have you eaten from the tree that I commanded you not to eat from?" (Genesis 3:11). In the same verse, He got them to face their shame: "Who told you that you were naked?" Finally, though they tried to shift the blame—Adam to Eve, and Eve to the serpent—He covered their shame and forgave them. He set them on a journey of restoration with the promise of an eventual Redeemer. He already had a plan for their healing.

God's antidote to shame is the gospel.

Do you remember what God says about our rebirth? "If anyone is in Christ, he is a new creature; the old things passed away; behold, new things have come" (2 Corinthians 5:17 NASB). The promise of a new creation puts our past in the past tense and our present and future as a process of all things becoming new. In other words, God's antidote to shame is the gospel.

The Eighteen-Inch Journey from Head to Heart

In the opening verses of Ephesians, Paul reminds believers of our new standing with God and the spiritual blessings we possess because of our relationship with Jesus. He emphasizes that we are *loved, chosen, wanted, adopted* by the Father into His family, *redeemed, valuable, secure,* and *sealed* with His Spirit. Then, after all of these amazing truths, he prays: Paul asks God to move these truths from the page of his letter to the minds of his readers and then finally into their hearts.

> I keep asking that the God of our Lord Jesus Christ, the glorious Father, may give you the Spirit of wisdom and revelation, so that you may know him better.

> I pray also that the eyes of your heart may be enlightened in order that you may know the hope to which he has called you, the riches of his glorious inheritance in his holy people, and his incomparably great power for us who believe.

> That power is the same as the mighty strength he exerted when he raised Christ from the dead and seated him at his right hand in the heavenly realms, far above all rule and authority, power and dominion, and every name that is invoked,

not only in the present age but also in the one to come. And God placed all things under his feet and appointed him to be head over everything for the church, which is his body, the fullness of him who fills everything in every way. (Ephesians 1:17–23)

Here Paul itemizes a series of requests that can be life-changing for all who pray them. He asks that God would give the Ephesians "the Spirit of wisdom and revelation"—insight and awareness, a glimpse of the divine plan and the power of God, an understanding of the deep truths of the gospel. He is asking that God would give them those "aha" moments by His Spirit so they can see into those truths about adoption and redemption and realize, *Oh, this is how it applies to me and the sin and shame of my past*. This spirit of revelation is an unveiling of the truth so that they would see it like never before and know God more personally and intimately.

He wants their view of God and themselves to change radically so they might experience Him as their Father and understand their value and worth. I pray this for my wife, children, grandchildren, and fellow workers on a regular basis. I paraphrase these verses and put their names in them, because I know that if they see and know God more deeply, all the other issues in their lives will fall into line.

After his request for wisdom and revelation, Paul prays that the eyes of their heart would be enlightened—that they would see things differently. Why? "In order that you may know . . . ," and then Paul outlines three things he wants his readers to know. For our lives to truly change, we need these three facts to sink into our hearts.

1. *"The hope to which he has called you."* This is our salvation. We use the word *hope* in a lot of ways—we hope it doesn't rain tomorrow, we hope our team wins the big game, we hope things work out between two people who have been going through a tough time. But when the Bible talks about hope, it's not just wishful thinking. Biblical hope is certain. It's looking forward to what is absolutely going to happen. The object of our hope is still in our future, but it's already a fact. So hope is an anticipation of what we know to be true: God's promises, a new heaven and earth, and the return of Jesus. The fact of our salvation is both a present reality and a future hope.

2. *"The riches of his glorious inheritance in his holy people."* This is a pretty full concept that we need to understand from several different angles. We know from Paul's letters that Jesus is the heir of all things (Colossians 1:16) and that we are coheirs with Him (Romans 8:17). So, if He stands to inherit all things and we are coheirs in His family, then we also stand to inherit all things. This is why Jesus could promise that the meek would inherit the earth (Matthew 5:5). We have entered into the inheritance of the Son.

That's part of what Paul means by "the riches of his glorious inheritance," but there's more. We also need to understand the riches of God's inheritance *in us,* "his holy people." I had a hard time putting this into words for years, but I think I understand it best through my own experience as a father. My children will receive an inheritance from me, but they also *are* my inheritance.

I have watched my children go through ups and downs, marry well, learn valuable skills, grow in character and Christ-likeness, and bring me inexpressible joy. The grandchildren they have given us are a treasure. This is my inheritance—the legacy that is passed on from generation to generation, with something of myself imparted to each one of them.

What if that's how God sees us? What if we really believed not only that we get an inheritance but that, as an absolute fact, we *are* the treasure of God? Imagine Him looking at us and saying, "You are My treasure, and I want you to believe that as a fact." That's what I think Paul means by "his glorious inheritance in his holy people." That's a vision that, when firmly planted in our hearts, makes shame a distant memory.

3. ***"His incomparably great power for us who believe."*** Because we're born of God's Spirit when we believe, we're filled with power. Paul gives three examples of how this power works.

First, it's the same power God used when He raised Jesus from the dead and seated Him in heavenly places. In other words, we live in and have access to the power of the resurrection and the authority of Jesus's exaltation to His heavenly throne. We can experience this resurrection power in our daily lives through the Spirit who lives within us, which puts us high above all classes of angels and principalities in God's hierarchy of beings, not only in this age, but also in the age to come.

Second, it's a power that comes because God placed all things under Jesus's feet. That's authority. Jesus is at the right hand of God, high above all other forces at work in this universe, and that authority is somehow part of the power we are given when we believe.

Finally, God appointed Jesus to be head over everything for the church, His body—the fullness of Him who fills everything in every way. Jesus's position gives us the power to win battles and overcome obstacles. When we think, *I can't break through the shame, I'll never be able to change, I'll never get over this addiction,* and we listen to all the self-talk that keeps us down, this is the power that has the potential to overcome. There is nothing that can hinder or inhibit our ability to live in the power of the resurrection and walk in supernatural strength.

> *There is nothing that can hinder or inhibit our ability to live in the power of the resurrection and walk in supernatural strength.*

In other words, guilt, shame, and every other debilitating condition we experience are futile in the face of the power at work within us. Paul might as well be saying, "Do you have any idea who you really are? Do you understand what God has given you?" He is convincing his readers, including us, that the greatest power in the universe is available to us as part of our salvation.

If that's true—if this supernatural power is at work inside every single person who has believed in Jesus and received His Spirit—then how do we tap into it to overcome shame, the fear of punishment or rejection, or the fear of death? What does this truth look like in our everyday lives?

How Do We Overcome True and False Shame?

We live in a time when shame is just a psychological term and almost always considered to be false or illegitimate. It's never your fault. But biblically speaking, true and false shame both exist.

True shame is the kind of shame that comes from falling short of God's standards—through our past failures, moral lapses, distorted desires like greed and lust, immoral behaviors, lies and manipulations, and everything else we have done that contradicts His character. It is good and right to feel a sense of grief or regret over these things, and they do indicate that something is fundamentally wrong with our fallen nature. His Word is clear about that: all have sinned and fallen short of His glory (Romans 3:23), and true shame attaches itself to that awareness.

But we also struggle with false shame that derives from standards that others have placed on us—parental demands we couldn't live up to, cultural standards or impossible social expectations, and even legalism or moralism within the Church devoid of grace. In fact, the Church can be one of the worst offenders in creating false guilt, which is perhaps one of the reasons the world rebels against holier-than-thou Christians.

Religion, regardless of the form it takes, often tries to control people through shame as a means of getting them to behave better. But shame is a horrible motivator and usually has the opposite effect. Shaming someone into doing the right thing rarely works for long.

So, how do we break through all of those forces—the genuine guilt and false distortions—that produce the shame we feel? Three critical approaches are embedded in this passage from Ephesians and echoed in many other parts of Scripture.

1. *Receive Christ.* That's the first answer to virtually everything in life, God's number one will for each of us. "To all who did receive him, to those who believed in his name, he gave the right to become children of God" (John 1:12). I believe that a lot of people who have begun to embrace Christian truth and biblical teaching are still on something of a self-improvement program; they put good principles into practice without making the decision to accept Christ.

But the gospel is not a self-improvement program; it's a rebirth. As is often said, Jesus didn't come to make us better; He came to make us new. There has to be a day and time when we recognize that we have sinned before a holy God and are in desperate need of a Savior. We confess that we haven't measured up, realize Jesus has paid the penalty, ask for His forgiveness, place our faith in Him, and ask Him to come into our lives as Lord to save and empower us to follow Him. If you haven't made that decision yet, I strongly encourage you to do so. Everything else depends on that.

2. *Ask the Father.* This is what Paul did in Ephesians when he wanted these truths to be real to his readers. He asked. He entered into a deep and meaningful conversation with the Father. That can be a challenge for many of us. Sometimes we don't know where to begin or how to put it into words, but the important thing is to begin. When I feel stuck and

I'm not sure how or what to pray for family and friends, I just follow Paul's model.

What do you think would happen if you prayed this way daily for the people in your life? You simply can put their names in the blanks: "Father, I ask that You give _____ a spirit of wisdom and revelation so that he/she might know You better; that the eyes of _____'s heart would be enlightened so he/she might know the hope of Your calling, the riches of Your glorious inheritance in Your holy people, and Your incomparably great power toward those who believe."

Jesus didn't come to make us better; He came to make us new.

Or consider simply asking God to help them understand who He is, that they would know they are *adopted*, *loved*, *redeemed*, and *sealed*, that they would get a glimpse of the amazing *love* and *power* that He offers. Those are powerful prayers that target all the guilt, shame, rejection, insecurities, and other junk going on in human hearts and minds. And we never need to tack on to the end of them, "Lord, if it's Your will." We know this is His will because He said so. God will answer that prayer.

3. Believe three historical facts. This passage in Ephesians addresses our past, present, and future. As we learn to believe what it says about our own chronology, we will experience progressive freedom from our shame and our fears.

First, *your past no longer defines you.* Paul wanted his readers to know about the certain hope of their calling. God has removed our sins from us as far as the east is from the west (Psalm

103:12). Too many Christians are still letting their past define them, even after years of following Jesus. They have never let their shame come to the surface, been honest about it, and let God work on it. It still seems too painful, so they bury it.

Theresa and Valerie brought their shame out in the open and allowed God to heal them of it and use it powerfully in the healing of others. They both quit hiding and refused to let their past dominate them. They became free in Christ.

You can activate that same freedom if you're willing, in a safe place, to bring that shame out of the shadows and open up about it. God is great at making His power visible in our weakness; He can turn your pain into healing and restoration for you and others. Who in your life is mature and safe enough to hear the secrets that hold you prisoner?

> *You are going to experience the ultimate happiness, and nothing can prevent that.*

Second, *your future happiness is guaranteed*. Think about the riches of God's inheritance. You are God's child, His treasure. That's guaranteed. You may have ups and downs, mistakes and disappointments, and all kinds of bumps and bruises in life. Your kids or your marriage, if you have them, may not turn out how you expected. Your business may fail. Still, you belong to God. You will meet Jesus. You will get a new body in a perfect environment and live with Him for all eternity. You are going to experience the ultimate happiness, and nothing can prevent that.

You can actually go ahead and live your life with the assumption that you cannot fail. You don't have to worry about what people think or be afraid of taking risks. You do not need to focus on self-protection or self-preservation. Your future is going to be awesome.

That's what Scripture tells us: "No eye has seen, no ear has heard, and no mind has imagined what God has prepared for those who love him" (1 Corinthians 2:9 NLT). In other words, your future is so good, so wonderful, and so awesome that you can't even comprehend it. If you're filled with anxiety about your future, lift up your eyes. Everything that concerns you is temporary, but your future happiness is forever. Sure, you'll have some struggles and setbacks—we all do. You live in a fallen world. But none of that can touch the future God has promised you.

Finally, *you have incomprehensible power to meet all your present challenges and opportunities.* That is a brief summary of the rest of Paul's prayer in Ephesians 1:19–23 when he goes on and on about the power of God in our lives. All of those examples of power—the power of the resurrection, the power that put Jesus above every power and every name, the power that fills everything with the presence of God—may be beyond our comprehension, but they are still available to us.

This power dwells inside of us.

Why Aren't We Experiencing It?

Are you accessing the power that dwells inside you?

Imagine that your car is broken down on a rural road in the middle of a snowstorm. And you went alone. So you're

147

shivering and wondering what to do next when you remember you passed a motel not too far back. You also remember that you don't have any cash and your phone battery is dead, so you can't call anyone or pay anyone to help. Even so, you begin walking back to the last signs of civilization.

Finally, you get to the intersection where the motel was, and you notice an ATM. Even though you don't have any cash or credit cards on you, you do have a healthy checking account and a bank card. What are you going to do? Will you continue to stand in the cold? Go back and sit in your car? Obviously, if you have a bank card, a full account, and access to an ATM, you're in business. You walk up to the machine, stick the card in, and withdraw some cash.

All your problems are overcome in that one simple transaction. You can get a room, call someone to help, pay for car repairs, eat a meal—whatever you need. All you had to do was appropriate what you already possessed.

That's what Ephesians is telling us: you have a power within you that can break through obstacles.

It is a supernatural strength, a practical energy, a muscular force that is stronger than dynamite and can break you free from the things that have held you prisoner for years. Whatever you experienced in your family of origin, whatever mistakes you've made, whomever you have offended, whatever labels have been attached to you, all you have to do is activate the power that is already available. You need to get out your spiritual ATM card and make the withdrawal.

How? The currency of God's kingdom is faith. That's how you get things in His economy, whether it's salvation, answers to prayer, a renewed mind, a changed heart, or anything else. The key to activating His promises and blessings is to believe. Just as you received the Lord, so walk in Him (Colossians 2:6). How did you receive Him? By faith. So, continue to live by faith, just as we are urged to do again and again on virtually every page of Scripture.

Faith is always rooted in the promises of God, and God's promises are in His Word. Peter wrote that we've been given everything we need to live a powerful, godly life—that God "has given us his very great and precious promises, so that through them you may participate in the divine nature" (2 Peter 1:4). When you get Word-centered and claim His promises, it's like taking withdrawals out of the bank. Sometimes you need other people drawing out of their ATMs too, so ask others to pray with you in unity for God's power to break through.

God's power often breaks through in surprising ways—not only by our asking and believing but frequently in the context of our weakness. Paul wrote often about the grace that was at work within him (1 Corinthians 15:10), the power of God made perfect in our weakness (2 Corinthians 12:9), the priceless treasure we carry in our earthen vessels (2 Corinthians 4:7). It may be hard to wrap our heads around that, but that power is ours as His sons and daughters.

Theresa and I look back at what God has done through a girl from a broken background and a skinny, insecure guy, and we can hardly believe how God has changed us and used us. Millions of people have heard what I teach and have been healed by hearing her story. I can assure you it's not because we had it all together and figured out how life works. Almost always, God's power has been manifested in our weakness.

There was a point when the lights came on and I realized, I am desperately insecure, and most of what I do is posing and posturing to please and impress other people. And I'm sick of it. And I went public with that. Theresa stopped hiding her painful background and the shame it brought her and went public with those secrets. I think something supernatural happens when we do that: God breaks in.

People get hopeful when they see others going through the same experiences they have had and wrestling with the same problems, and I'm convinced we have more authority in our lives by being honest about our weaknesses.

I know people who have made major mistakes and have gone through serious challenges in their past, but their own children don't know anything about those struggles. The parents are ashamed of how they used to live, so they project a false image to their kids of never having had any real problems. They tell their children how they need to live. But it can be much more powerful to confess struggles with alcohol or promiscuity or bad decisions and how much pain they brought.

There's a right and a wrong time and way to share those things, and I don't believe in embarrassing people with too much information. But the power of God is released when we say, "Lord, I need You. I'm going to be honest and authentic, and I'm trusting You to use that to give hope to other people's lives."

If you're stuck in your shame, you'll probably stay there or experience minimal change until you can release it in a safe place, at the right time, with people who will handle your pain with care. It might feel risky to expose your secrets—to tell someone you were abused as a child or stole something or are addicted to pornography. But if you do that wisely with people who really care about you, God will show up and you will experience real change in your life. That has certainly been true in our journey as a couple, and we are not an exception. It's the journey of every believer.

If you truly long to change, it'll mean consistently engaging with God's Word and getting involved in authentic, non-judgmental relationships with other believers at a heart-to-heart level. These are two prerequisites for transformation. Unfortunately, neither is common among most Christians. The power of God shows up in the lives of Word-centered, promise-believing, fellowship-focused people.

In everything, faith is the key. It's the only currency in God's economy. It can move mountains, please God, and be the catalyst for miracles. So, now is your time to experience His power. Pray with confidence. Choose to believe the truth about your past, present, and future. Take steps of faith in what God has done and continues to do by the power of His Spirit. It's how you started your Christian life and how you can live each and every day.

How to See Yourself as God Sees You

The reason God is so adamant about our knowing we are *loved*, *wanted*, *competent*, *valuable*, and *secure* is not only so we can be happier and more fulfilled. That's certainly part of His purpose for us; Jesus came so that our "joy may be complete" (John 15:11).

But we can't experience His joy fully if we don't also realize another purpose for receiving His love. We are His body, and He has transformed us to be His instruments, His ambassadors, His agents who share His love with others. People need to know that Christ died for them, that He rose from the dead, and that they don't have to go to hell one day—or live in a hell today.

They can only know there is a Father who loves them if our lives and words communicate that story boldly and compassionately. Many have turned the message around to prioritize superficial happiness and self-improvement over the message of eternal salvation. It's all about personal fulfillment and material prosperity in the here and now. But God is interested in ultimate joy for the long term, for you and everyone else.

Replacing our warped mirrors and misbeliefs with the truth of God's Word begins here. God secured our salvation and blessed us with every spiritual blessing in Christ in order to transform us. Part of that transformation is being His mouthpiece, His hands, and His feet to demonstrate His love to others. We can't do that when we are trapped in shame.

Shame over time creates misbeliefs that get rooted deeply in our hearts. We come to believe that we have little to offer God and others and that change is impossible. Below are two common lies that must be exposed along with a complementary truth to remind us we are indeed competent in Christ.

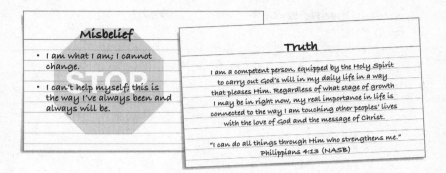

It's true—no matter how you may feel, you are competent. Philippians 4:13 assures you that you can do all things through Christ who strengthens you. God would not give you such amazing promises and call you to serve Him without equipping you to believe His Word and fulfill your calling. At your core, you're exactly who He made you to be, and you've been given everything you need to live a godly life and be used by Him to love others. As you do, your shame can be used to bring Him fame.

That's the pattern in Scripture and in the thousands of people who have gone into training by reviewing these cards. As you renew your mind with these truths, you will experience greater and greater freedom, and many will be blessed by God's power manifesting through your weakness.

Take some time now to read the following questions slowly and reflectively. Shame is a big and deep issue, and we've covered a lot of material in this chapter. Let God speak to you gently through His Spirit.

▬▬▬ Questions for Reflection and Discussion ▬▬▬

1) If shame is so devastating, is there anything more powerful? According to John 3:16, what is it?

2) If the gospel is God's antidote to shame and has the power to radically change lives, why are Christians still living in shame?

3) Could believing that you will not only receive an inheritance from God but that you *are* His inheritance change the way you see shame? How?

4) The three critical steps to breaking through genuine guilt and false distortions are:

- Receive Christ (John 1:12)
- Ask the Father (Ephesians 1:17–23)
- Believe the three historical facts (Psalm 103:12)

  » Your past no longer defines you (see p. 145)— Psalm 103:12
  » Your future happiness is guaranteed (see p. 146)—1 Corinthians 2:9
  » You have incomprehensible power to meet all your present challenges and opportunities (see p. 147)—1 Corinthians 15:10

  Where are you in relation to these three steps? Ask God to help you take that next step toward Him.

5) What is faith? Faith is always rooted in the promises of God, and God's promises are in His Word. How can you grow in your faith?

154

6) There is healing, hope, and power in telling others your testimony. Although you may be nervous and unsure, tell your story to a safe friend this week. Tell your friend what God has done in your life.

A Deeper Look at Paul's Prayer

Paul's prayer in Ephesians 1 is both a plea for truth to move from our heads to our hearts and a model of how it can. We need wisdom and revelation to grasp the blessings Paul presented in the first chapter, and we need to step into the hope of our calling, the riches of God's inheritance, and the power of faith. This journey from head to heart is all about knowing, both in purpose and in process.

There are two words for *to know* in Greek. When Paul prays for a spirit of wisdom and revelation in the knowledge of God, he implies a personal experience, the knowledge that comes only from intimate relational connection. He is praying that his readers would know God and His blessings in the depths of their soul and feel them with the emotional intensity they deserve.

The grammar of verse 18 suggests a completed fact: that the eyes of your heart, having been enlightened, might know . . . It has already occurred. That's because the moment we receive Christ, the eyes of our hearts—not just our minds— begin to open. We see things differently. It's a process, but we now have the capacity to see the truth.

The prayer then turns when Paul prays that the eyes of our hearts would be enlightened in order *to know* . . . This use of "know" employs another Greek verb; it's the word for understanding objective facts. This kind of knowledge is not personal and relational but entirely about absolutes. In the context of experiential knowledge of God, he prays for our objective knowledge of three things that need to sink into our hearts: "the hope to which he has called you," "the riches of his glorious inheritance in his holy people," and "his incomparably great power for us who believe." (Ephesians 1:18-19 NIV) These three facts radically change our lives.

Paul's language crescendos throughout this prayer as he tries to express the inexpressible and climaxes in his description of God's power. The extent of the power within us is beyond what we can imagine. It's available to everyone who believes in Jesus, and we experience it as we exercise faith in the situations we face and the prayers we pray.

The word for power here is *dunamis,* the same word that was later used for dynamite when it was invented. This *dunamis* power has several connotations, including the power of armies, the supernatural power needed for miracles, and the basic power of the will to live with excellence and exert influence. This power is everything we need to overcome every obstacle in our past, present, or future.

In "the working of the strength of His might" (v. 19 NASB), Paul also uses an expressive word for how this power functions. *Energeo* is the root from which we derive our English word "energy." It is operational power—not just capacity or potential but the kind of power that makes things happen and brings about change. The word for "might" is often used for bodily strength or muscular force, and the word for "strength" is the power to overcome obstacles, resistance, or control. So, Paul's vocabulary in these verses is a package of power terms, a cluster of words that should leave the reader with the impression that there is nothing that can hinder or inhibit our ability to live in the power of the resurrection and walk in supernatural strength.

Every debilitating condition we experience is futile in the face of the power at work within us.

PART 5

BEAUTIFUL

9

The Lie of Guilt

When he was in the middle of high school, my dad felt compelled to help defend America in World War II after the attack on Pearl Harbor. He was only sixteen and a half and had to have his mother sign the enlistment papers. He was a strong and gifted athlete, so they made him a .50-caliber machine gunner.

Later in life, in a rare moment of reflection, Dad shared the horrors of Guam and Iwo Jima where he'd killed thousands. My father survived, because he was wounded at Iwo Jima, but none of his unit made it out alive.

He bore the guilt of things he'd done, and he felt a false guilt for surviving when none of his buddies made it out alive. He tried to quiet his guilt with heavy drinking, but sometimes he'd still have outbursts of anger. To the outside world, alcohol and anger issues looked like his biggest problems. But behind those manifestations, his core problem was a gnawing, crushing guilt, and he had no idea how to deal with it.

Shame and guilt go hand in hand, one feeding the other. They are partners of destruction, eroding our lives. And as we do with shame, most of us carry guilt around for years. Few emotions can distort our mirror and make us feel as dirty, ugly, unworthy, and unlovable as guilt does. And we all struggle with it—no exceptions.

Examining the Universal Problem

Where have you struggled with guilt in your life? Ephesians 2 explains the root of our problem with guilt and God's solution for it. It isn't just a little problem; it goes much deeper than most of us imagine.

> As for you, you were *dead* in your *transgressions* and *sins*, in which you used to live when you followed the ways of this world and of the *ruler of the kingdom* of the air, the spirit who is now at work in those who are *disobedient*. All of us also lived among them at one time, gratifying the cravings of our flesh and following its desires and thoughts. Like the rest, we were by nature *deserving of wrath*. (Ephesians 2:1–3)

When Paul writes "as for you," he is referring to Gentiles, people outside of God's covenant, unaware of God's law and His nature, living according to their own designs. When he writes "all of us" in verse 3, he is including all of humanity, Jew and Gentile, who were trapped in a sinful nature, gratifying lustful, self-centered desires. The human condition is not selective; it applies to us all. We all have a serious problem at our core.

Notice the extreme vocabulary Paul uses here: "dead," "disobedient," "deserving of wrath." The word *dead* literally means "separated," harking back to God's warning in Genesis that, in the day human beings first sinned, we would surely die. Adam and Eve died—not physically yet, but spiritually, separated from God. They continued to live for many years, but they couldn't reconnect with God. Sin separates us from Him, and there is nothing we can do on our end to reestablish that relationship. The only remedy is divine intervention.

We were dead in our transgressions and sins, Paul says. The word for *sin* means "missing the mark," and originally was used to describe someone throwing a spear or shooting an arrow that fell short of its target. We have all repeatedly missed the mark.

We are therefore alienated from God. We followed the ways of the world, fitting into a culture that is by nature hostile to God—one that is more in keeping with Satan, the "ruler of the kingdom of the air," than with the kingdom of God. In this alternate, rebel culture, people treat each other in ungodly ways, grow comfortable in their disobedience, and develop a new normal in which manipulation, envy, injury, and abuse are commonplace and even expected.

We see this on a large scale, don't we? The genocides, terrorist movements, tyrannies, rampant abortions, drive-by shootings, racism, and the slander of entire groups of people. All of these—as well as the more minor personal insults and selfishness we experience—are clear evidence of a world in rebellion against God.

Paul is simply saying that humanity has lived in this kind of disobedience from the beginning, cultivating an alternate kingdom that's hostile to His ways and caters to the self. The passions, cravings, lusts, and self-gratifying behaviors that we've inherited since Eden make us objects of God's wrath. He hates evil, and as a holy and just God, He has to punish it. As much as He loves us, we fall under that punishment because of our sin.

G. K. Chesterton, the British journalist and theological thinker who had such a huge impact on C. S. Lewis, was once asked, "What is wrong with the world?" His answer to that question was profound: "I am." Not the government, not advancing weapon technology, not Germany's new political star named Hitler, but himself. In other words, everyone is. The problems of the world begin in the human heart.

Theologians have a term for this condition: *total depravity*. It doesn't mean we're all as bad as we can possibly be—most people, after all, try to make the right choices and do some pretty good things. It means that sin is universal, infecting every human heart. Contrary to what we've been told, human beings are not basically good. Most of us try to be good, but we inevitably turn away from God. The solution, therefore, is not more education, the right environment, better technology, equitable distribution of goods, or some utopia when everyone will just cooperate. Our efforts at a better society aren't enough. They don't fix our fundamental problem.

Paul wrote in Romans, "Just as sin entered the world through one man, and death through sin, and in this way death came to all people, because all sinned" (Romans 5:12). In other words, we're born into sin. We don't have to teach our kids to be selfish; they know by default. As they grow up, they learn some unselfish ways—and more sophisticated ways to mask their selfishness. We all do that. We each have a tendency to seek our self-interests when we can.

The prophet Jeremiah wrote some scathing words about the human heart. He said, "The heart is deceitful above all things and beyond cure" (Jeremiah 17:9). He also prophesied that we would receive a new heart, and as we've seen, we can receive it

> *Contrary to what we've been told, human beings are not basically good. Most of us try to be good, but we inevitably turn away from God.*

as part of our salvation. But in our original condition, he was right about our deceitfulness. *We are stuck in a helpless condition.*

God's commentary on the root of our problems is a far cry from what I was taught in high school, college, and graduate school. What about you? Do you believe that we are born sinful and utterly helpless? Most people, even Christians, do not. We tend to think we're better off than that and just need a little help. We're looking for self-improvement, not a resurrection. But our sin puts us beyond self-help. The consequence of disobedience is death and destruction. That's how far down our guilt goes, and until we face our problems—the root of them, not just the symptoms—and see that we're separated from God, we will not seek His solution. We'll continue to live in futility and frustration—and under judgment.

Understanding the Complexity of Guilt

Guilt has been called the most destructive of all emotions. Let me ask you: Are you wrestling with guilt? If so, even if it's a subtle, nagging feeling, I'd encourage you to whisper a prayer and ask God to give you the courage and strength to be honest with yourself and with Him. He wants to help you, and He can. Removing our guilt is at the heart of the gospel. That's why Jesus came.

Guilt is tricky. It usually doesn't manifest as guilt. It shows up in all the relational issues, personal struggles, distorted perspectives, and misplaced motivations and desires we have. Guilt is a root cause that rarely comes to the surface, but the root feeds the whole tree. Sometimes our guilt is true, that is, based on what we have actually done, but sometimes it's false, the product of demands others have placed on us, ideals we have held, and a nagging feeling that we don't measure up.

> *Guilt is a root cause that rarely comes to the surface, but the root feeds the whole tree.*

Despite my dad's good intentions, I learned to feel guilty if I wasn't productive every minute of every day. Achievement, success, and work were the mantras of my childhood. I felt false guilt when I stopped, relaxed, or took a breath. By contrast, true guilt, theological guilt, applies to all of us: all have sinned and fallen short of God's glory. But the way we see our guilt and the ways we deal with it are very often inaccurate. So, before we go any further, let's look at what guilt really is.

What Is Guilt?

The *literal* meaning of the word *guilt* is the state of having committed an offense. It's the opposite of innocence. It means you have done something wrong; you've violated a standard. If you violated a human standard, it may be *relative* guilt—something that's wrong to some people but not to others. If you violated a divine standard, it's *absolute* guilt—something that's wrong for all people at all times, like murder, stealing, envy, greed, pride. But in every case, it's missing the mark of a standard or ideal.

The *psychological* meaning of guilt is a little different. In common usage today, this psychological definition focuses on the emotional response and the perception of having broken a rule or fallen short of an expectation—even if this feeling doesn't correspond with reality. As psychologist Becca Johnson writes, it's "an emotional response to the perception that we have broken a prohibition or fallen short of a standard. Thus, guilt can be both a fact and a feeling, and the two are not necessarily related."[1]

You can feel free of guilt and be very guilty. Sociopaths kill people without feeling any guilt or remorse, but they're certainly guilty before God and the law. On a far smaller scale, some of us violate the law of the land (think speed limits and tax itemizations) or the rules of an organization (fudging time sheets or stealing office supplies) and feel no guilt or remorse at all because we don't agree with the rules or think our offenses are trivial. Here's my point: you don't have to *feel* guilty to *be* guilty. Some of us do this even with the clear commands in Scripture, because they don't feel right to us or relevant to our lives.

> *You don't have to **feel** guilty to **be** guilty.*

Many self-identifying Christ followers in the twenty-first century no longer believe the command to remain sexually pure before marriage applies to them. They may not feel guilt, but in fact they are guilty before God and will experience the consequences of their actions. By contrast, you can feel very guilty and not be guilty at all. When I sit down and relax, I have to fight feelings of guilt. Others have far more serious false guilt; they are victims of abuse and feel guilty for something someone else did to them, as if they were somehow responsible. That's a tragic psychological trick, but millions have been dealing with this false guilt for years. In order to address our guilt, we have to discern the difference between true and false guilt, which we'll look at a little more closely in the next chapter.

The *theological* meaning of guilt focuses on absolutes, not feelings or perceptions. It is the moral and legal condition of all people prior to receiving Christ's gift of salvation by faith. It reflects our personal accountability and just condemnation for sin and transgressions against God's law. God is holy and perfect, and in order to have a relationship with Him, we must be holy and perfect too. But we aren't. We have all sinned, and we all bear the guilt of our sins until we receive Christ (see Romans 3:9–23 for a clear statement about our sinfulness). When we come to faith in Him, He takes our sin on Himself, and we receive His forgiveness. Apart from that relationship, all humanity is guilty.

But God, out of His great love, obliterated our guilt by placing it on Christ. If you're a genuine follower of Jesus, you have no guilt before God. Romans 8:1 says, "There is now no condemnation for those who are in Christ Jesus." So why, you might ask, do you still feel so guilty? The answer is twofold. First, even after we come to Christ, we carry with us the false guilt and baggage of our past. Second, we all commit sins after our initial experience of salvation. This short-circuits our fellowship with the Lord, and the Holy Spirit lets us know. That conviction expresses itself in feelings of guilt but, unlike condemnation, has the sole purpose of restoration and reconnection with the Lord.

> *In order to address our guilt, we have to discern the difference between true and false guilt.*

How Do You Tend to Cope with Guilt?

In her book *Good Guilt, Bad Guilt*, Becca Johnson observes that there are things we feel guilty *about* and things we feel guilty *because of*. Things we feel guilty *about* might include decisions like eating the wrong things or not eating the right things, wasting time, gaining weight, making a bad financial decision, relaxing, taking a vacation, procrastinating, being lazy or undisciplined, forgetting to call Mom or email the boss or return a message. Or we may feel guilty about habits like smoking or nail biting, not exercising enough, watching too much TV, or not praying or reading the Bible enough.

But we can also feel guilty *because of* negative attitudes or ongoing behaviors, such as having an affair, struggling with lust or pornographic fantasies, stealing from work, or compulsively lying or gambling. The list could go on and on, of course, but regardless of the specific cause, most of us have some kind of guilt eating away at us.

How do we deal with that? Usually in unhealthy ways. We tend to do exactly what our first parents did. First, we hide it. Then we deny it or excuse it. Then we blame other people: "I wouldn't be on the internet if my wife were more affectionate." "If they paid me a decent salary, I wouldn't have to make up for it on my own." "I'm only this way because of how my parents treated me." Even when our guilt is pointing the finger inward, we justify our attitudes and actions to ourselves and others by pointing the finger outward. Blame is one way of trying to strip our guilt of its power, but it never works.

We all have a drug of choice to cover our guilt. Mine is work. I was told year after year that I was a workaholic, but I responded with denial after denial, excuse after excuse, continually shifting the blame. And I kept on working.

One day I walked into a bookstore and saw a title that stopped me in my tracks. I didn't even read the book, just the title: *I Feel Guilty When I Relax*. I thought, *That's me!* I realized my workaholism and desperate attempts to cover it up were nothing but guilt. I went on a painful journey of learning to be honest with myself, God, and the people around me to bring my unresolved guilt to the surface. Some of it was true, some was false, and all of it needed to be dealt with. It was a difficult process but a good one.

Your drug of choice may be entirely different from mine, but it still needs to be dealt with. Is it shopping? Food? Entertainment? An addiction? A medication? Something else? If you aren't sure what it is, you'll notice it beginning to surface whenever you feel restless, start to reflect on your problems, think about the big issues of life, or are reminded of past mistakes or dysfunctional patterns. Your instinct will be to bury the guilt and turn to your distraction, your "drug." But if you bury your memories and your guilt, they'll continue to fester. As a pastor I've watched it happen to countless people, and it never leads to a good outcome.

The good news is that God has a comprehensive solution for our guilt, and it's extremely effective. But in order to take advantage of it, we have to be honest. Denying our symptoms, like I did for years with my workaholism, doesn't lead us to His solution. We first have to identify the symptoms and behaviors; then we can explore the guilt that creates them. When we do, God begins a healing process that not only removes the symptoms but deals with the cause. In the next chapter, we'll discover Christ's solution so our souls can finally live in peace.

══ Questions for Reflection and Discussion ══

1) Do you see yourself as precious and beautiful in God's eyes? What adjectives would you use to describe yourself?

2) As God's child, what are some of the adjectives God would use to describe you?

3) When asked what was wrong with the world, G. K. Chesterton answered, "I am." Do you think the prophet Jeremiah would agree? (See Jeremiah 17:9.) Would today's popular culture agree? Why or why not?

4) When coping with guilt, people hide it, bury it, deny it, excuse it, justify it, or blame others for it. Do you find yourself dealing with guilt in one or more of these ways? Which ones?

5) What is theological guilt? What is false guilt?

6) Read Romans 8:1: "Therefore, there is no condemnation for those who are in Christ Jesus." As one who is in Jesus, should you feel guilt or condemnation? Then why do we?

10

You Are Beautiful

Ephesians 2:1–10

In many respects, my father was an amazing man. He was good-looking, intelligent, and well-educated and had a charming personality. He was an all-star high school and college athlete; he was offered a pro baseball contract upon finishing college, and he won the state of Virginia Golden Gloves boxing championship upon returning from the war. In addition, he captured the heart of a beautiful young woman who became my mom. It would not be an overstatement to say that he was greatly blessed by God with a beautiful life.

Tragically, my father's unresolved guilt ate at his soul like a cancer. As I've mentioned, he tried to drown it through alcohol—first just a little, then more and more until it overcame him. That was his problem, but not his alone. There is no such thing as private sin or guilt. They always affect other people.

In an alcoholic's family, there's usually a scapegoat, an enabler, and a rescuer, among other roles. My oldest sister was the scapegoat. Dad didn't treat her well, and she eventually rebelled. My other sister was the compliant one, often invisible and always trying to keep the peace. She cooked meals, helped out any way she could, and developed an eating disorder. My role was the rescuer. My father would drink all day on Saturdays, and whenever he stepped out of the room, I would take his drink and pour it down the drain. I thought I was helping. My mom was the enabler—emotionally intelligent but with few boundaries and convictions, until Dad's couple of beers after work turned into missing supper and eventually not coming home until late at night. Only then did Mom do something to turn the family around.

When Mom finally realized she was the enabler and that Dad's drinking was destroying the family, she did something really brave. She established boundaries and set up what you could call an intervention. She was a counselor, and she'd been married to this hard-charging but charming man for over twenty years. She was committed to the marriage and loved Dad very much, but she'd been loyal to a fault. Finally, she faced the hard truth: his behavior was destroying others and he needed help.

I remember that moment. I can still see Mom holding up a bottle of beer in front of Dad and saying, "You can have this, or you can have me and the kids. But you can't have both. You have to choose. You've got forty-eight hours."

Dad was a Marine and a math teacher, so he approached his answer very practically and logically. He quit drinking. In fact, he did more. He thought, *I drink a lot of beer and smoke three and a half packs of cigarettes every day. Might as well quit them both.* And he did.

After three months, I actually wanted him to drink another beer. He was a lot easier to live with when sedated by alcohol. He and our family hadn't dealt with any of his issues or ours, and he was driving us crazy. He didn't understand his guilt. It took him a long time to realize that he couldn't solve his problems on his own. No amount of willpower or positive thinking could bring him peace.

Dad's symptom was alcoholism, but as we've seen, guilt can manifest in a multitude of ways in our lives—shopping, money, work, sex, a relationship, a child's success, a spouse's behavior, a standard of living, an inflated ego, and more. All of these are symptoms. The real issue is guilt.

What Is God's Antidote for Guilt?

So, what does God want us to do with our guilt? The good news is that He doesn't want you to live with guilt, and He has an antidote for it.

God wants you to know that guilt is a formidable and complex foe. He wants you to be able to discern the difference between true and false guilt and to understand the danger of feeling guilty when you shouldn't—or the even greater danger of not feeling guilty when you should. He wants to remove it all—legally, authentically, permanently. Consider this good news from Ephesians 2:

> But because of his great love for us, God, who is rich in mercy, made us alive *with Christ* even when we were dead

in transgressions—it is by grace you have been saved. And God raised us up *with Christ* and seated us with him in the heavenly realms *in Christ Jesus*, in order that in the coming ages he might show the incomparable riches of his grace, expressed in his kindness to us *in Christ Jesus*. (Ephesians 2:4–7)

After describing our desperate condition in stark, discouraging terms, Paul quickly transitions with a very significant "but." It's like a bright, flashing red light that stops us where we are and says, "Yes, that negative assessment is definitely true, but there's another factor in the equation."

That factor is the hinge in this passage and in all of human history, the major theme of Scripture.

God, who is rich in mercy, loves us deeply and relentlessly. He will not leave us in our sinful condition. When we were dead in our transgressions—in our hostile rebellion against Him—He made us alive with Christ.

Then Paul gets excited about the almost unimaginable truth that comes next: "God raised us up with Christ and seated us with him in the heavenly realms" (v. 6). Why? So that in coming ages He might demonstrate the enormity and richness of His grace through Jesus. In other words, our salvation reveals something about God that could not have been seen otherwise: His incomprehensible mercy and grace toward the least likely creatures to deserve it.

Notice the recurring context throughout the entire passage: "with Christ" twice and "in Christ Jesus" twice. None of this happens apart from Jesus. We were dead without Him and trapped in disobedience, deserving God's righteous wrath and condemnation. But God isn't content with that as an end to the story. In His great mercy, He sent Jesus. Every blessing we receive, every promise God gives us, is always in Christ, with Christ, and through Christ.

Also, notice the way Scripture contrasts our former condition with our new one: we were dead but are now made alive.

The word "made alive" here means *to quicken*. We were spiritually dead, but the moment we received Christ, we were made alive and reconnected with the Father. We were co-resurrected with Jesus. Though we once walked in disobedience, we now walk in righteousness. "We were therefore buried with him through baptism into death in order that, just as Christ was raised from the dead through the glory of the Father, we too may live a new life" (Romans 6:4). We have a new kind of power working within us—not the power of sin but the power of the resurrection. We are being remade into something *entirely new*.

And finally, instead of destruction, we are seated with Jesus in heavenly places (v. 6). We've been enthroned. We were under the ruler of this world, but now we are above him and every other ruler and principality. We were once in the kingdom of darkness, but now we are in the kingdom of light.

Though the ruler of this world orchestrates his strategies through human flesh and selfishness, we've been raised and exalted with Jesus above these things. That's why God sees us differently now.

We are *wanted, secure, valuable, competent,* and, yes, even *beautiful*.

Former condition	New reality
Dead	Alive
Captive to the ruler of this world	Seated above in heavenly places
Objects of wrath	Objects of mercy
Following the world's ways	Living by faith
Gratifying sinful desires	Doing good works

Jesus intervened. He rescued us from condemnation and brought us into His family. That not only has applications to the big picture but also to the problems we face here and now. Jesus is the only answer for peace in this world, and He is the only answer for peace in our hearts.

Jesus is the reason my mother was able to stage an intervention for my father, boldly and lovingly give him an ultimatum. That's hard to do if you aren't sure God is going to take care of you regardless of what happens. And it's hard to challenge someone as guilt-ridden as my father was if you aren't convinced that Jesus can handle the enormity of that guilt.

I believe my mom's intervention is a small picture of what God does for us. While we are in a desperate and helpless situation, God, because of His great love, gives us a solution in Christ.

God's motive. Ephesians 2 clearly explains that God's motive for His intervention in our lives was love (v. 4). He didn't rescue us because we're special or wonderful or nice—though in His eyes that original design and potential are in all of us—or because we deserved it. He rescued us because He loves us. He's good to us not because we're good but because He is good.

God's action. Instead of death, we receive life. Instead of disobedience, we walk in newness and power. Instead of destruction in our future, we have hope for our future. His intervention met us at multiple points of need and redefined us, restoring us to the real selves He originally designed.

God's purpose. God's underlying purpose in saving us was to demonstrate and reveal who He is. You may have never realized this, but you are God's trophy. We were fallen, hurting people stuck in destructive patterns, but we were also victims of abuses, difficulties, and pain. As both the offenders and the offended, we were trapped in a world system that kept recycling the same suffering over again. But God's intervention changes that. It lifts us out. Salvation is freely given and full of more than enough grace and power to deliver us.

> *Jesus intervened. He rescued us from condemnation and brought us into His family.*

Let me ask you a personal question: *Why do you do what you do?* Be honest. Why do you keep pushing and striving for ways to sedate your pain or stimulate your pleasures to mask it? And why do you settle for substitutes? Why do you try to compensate for guilt on your own? And how well has your approach worked?

For years, I promised Theresa that I wouldn't work so many hours. None of those efforts and promises were effective until I realized the *why* behind my behavior. I was carrying a load of guilt. Deep down I felt like I didn't measure up. I was trying to earn God's love and forgiveness and get people to like and admire me. It was when I answered the *why* question that change began to occur.

God has solved my problem and yours. His solution is not a Band-Aid, a little bit of improvement, or a temporary fix. He intervened in order to eradicate and obliterate our guilt, not just hypothetically, theologically, and abstractly, but at the experiential level of our emotions and our everyday lives. He's given us everything we need to be free.

Experiencing God's Provision

Everything you've just read is true, and most Christ followers have a general idea that Jesus paid for their sins. But rare are the Christians who actually experience the freedom and peace from guilt that God has provided.

Consider the next verses we encounter in Ephesians 2:

> For it is by grace you have been saved, through faith—and this is not from yourselves, it is the gift of God—not by works, so that no one can boast. (Ephesians 2:8–9)

Remember that faith is the currency of God's kingdom. And this is a critical point—no amount of trying hard, extra effort, willpower, self-discipline, or pulling yourself up by your bootstraps is going to save you.

God does not help those who help themselves; He helps those who receive His help by faith. That is the reason no one can boast about salvation. Grace is the free, unmerited love of God that put Jesus on the cross to pay for our sins.

All the punishment you deserved was placed on Jesus, who cried out with the pains of abandonment because the Father turned away from Him. He took your condemnation to the grave with Him, where it stayed even after He rose from the dead and was exalted to heaven. Just as you received an inheritance of sin from all the past generations of human history, you now receive the righteousness of Christ. You're now God's son or daughter.

Our restoration can only begin when we recognize the full extent of our need. I think a lot of people go to church to be a better person—to raise their kids the right way, enjoy the music, have an uplifting experience, and be motivated by the messages.

But a person who takes that approach is missing the point. It's almost like praying, "Lord, please help me so my life can go the way I think it should, because my plan for my own fulfillment is a good one." That kind of request comes from someone who doesn't realize he or she

Most Christ followers have a general idea that Jesus paid for their sins. But rare are the Christians who actually experience the freedom and peace from guilt that God has provided.

has crossed a line and needs the gift of salvation. It assumes that completely surrendering to God might not work out well. But God's plans are always best for us, and we can't experience them unless we realize how desperately we need Him.

The source: 100 percent grace. I was in a checkout line recently at a big discount store and noticed the family behind me, a couple with a small child. They were clearly struggling financially. They were trying to figure out which items to put on the checkout belt, because they weren't quite sure they could pay for all their groceries. So, when I was paying, I whispered to the clerk to put their purchase on my card. The husband heard me and said, "What!? What are you doing?"

"It's okay, man. I've been blessed and want to share it with you. I'd be honored if you'd let me pay for your groceries."

"No, no, no." He was adamant. He wouldn't let me.

Why would anyone turn down more than $100 worth of groceries? He needed the help. He knew it, too. But I heard him talking to his wife about how he could do this himself; he didn't need anyone's charity, and on and on about himself. It was pride—all about him. He couldn't receive a free gift.

A lot of people are like that with salvation. Why would anybody turn down such an extravagant gift? They want to be in control. Human nature wants self-sufficiency, and God will allow that. He won't force His gift on anyone, just like I couldn't force my gift on this family. Their rebuff hurt my feelings, and I think our rejection of God's gift hurts His too. He wants us to have His best for our lives, and we can't get it on our own. We have to become like children—humble, open, and recognizing our need.

So how about you? What are you holding on to? What is keeping you from receiving all God wants to give you? I assure you the benefits are well worth the sacrifice.

The reception: through faith. We are saved by grace, but notice the only aspect of this transaction that is our responsibility: it's *through faith.* You trust, you believe, and you transfer your faith in yourself or something else back to God. You admit to Him that you need His help and ask Him for His solution. That's how salvation comes.

My father finally got to that point. He only overcame his guilt when he was able to say, "I can't do this myself." For a year after Mom's intervention, he didn't drink or smoke. I bet he went through a thousand packs of gum, because he had to do something to replace his old habits. I remember him asking me one day how I got this peace that he'd observed after I'd come to know Christ.

"I don't know, Dad. I just started reading the Bible." I was a believer, but not a very informed one.

So, being a good Marine, he got up at 5:00 a.m. to read the Bible every day. He kept reading through the Gospels. One day he said, "I'm not sure, but whatever you have has something to do with faith."

"Yeah, Dad," I said. "I think it has everything to do with faith."

This big Marine with advanced degrees and a family that looked pretty good on the outside was slowly coming to grips with having a family that included an alcoholic, an enabler, a rebellious child, a compliant child, an eating disorder, a rescuer, and a whole lot of pain. After six months of reading the New Testament, by God's grace, Dad found a copy of the "Four Spiritual Laws" tract. The Lord opened his eyes and heart, and he knelt down at the end of his bed.

"Lord Jesus," he said, "I have sinned against You. I've done many things wrong, and I've killed thousands of people. I can't imagine how You could forgive me. But Your Word says that You died in my place, so I'm asking You now, will You forgive me and come into my life?"

He had beaten the alcohol and tobacco, but he had never beaten the guilt until the day he trusted Christ. An amazing journey started, and even though there were a lot of ups and downs, it radically changed his life.

> *He had beaten the alcohol and tobacco, but he had never beaten the guilt until the day he trusted Christ.*

What about you? Have you ever put your trust in Christ? That's not the same as asking if you believe the gospel is true. Have you personally received Jesus as your Savior? If you haven't, please don't waste any more time trying to get over your problems and cover your guilt. Don't refuse His help. Bow your head and ask Him for the amazing, comprehensive gift of salvation.

The result: no condemnation. Paul makes an emphatic statement in Romans 8:1: "There is now no condemnation for those who are in Christ Jesus." You may *feel* guilt, but you don't actually have any—not from any legal or theological perspective. In Jesus, all your guilt has been paid for.

So why, you might ask, do you still feel guilty? Because there is a huge difference between condemnation and conviction. *Condemnation* points the finger at you and says, "You are a bad person. You deserve punishment." Scripture is very clear that the author of condemnation is the enemy of our souls. Satan is the accuser of the brethren (Revelation 12:10).

The goal of condemnation is to make you feel unworthy. It says you shouldn't get close to God, because He wouldn't want anything to do with you. It puts a false wall of division between you and God, insisting that He is very upset about what you've done and the kind of person you are. Sometimes it will come up as a condemning voice in your own thoughts: *You're a terrible parent. You're a terrible friend. You just can't get it right no matter how hard you try, can you?* Those thoughts come from the enemy, not from God.

By contrast, *conviction* comes from God. Conviction never says you're a bad person. It says you had a bad thought or did a bad thing. It separates you from your action because, after all, you are still a son or daughter of the King. It prompts you not to run away from God but to run toward Him—to confess your sin, turn away from it, receive God's forgiveness, and restore fellowship with your heavenly Father. It is authored by the Holy Spirit for your good.

Conviction is usually very specific: *Son/daughter, your attitude of unforgiveness is wrong, and it will destroy your relationship. That website you looked at is not good for you. That thing you said hurt your friend. You need to deal with that.* This gentle instruction comes so you can correct your mistakes and live in freedom. There's no reason to hide from conviction, look for excuses, or blame someone else. Your guilt has been dealt with. God just wants you to have the best possible life with healthy relationships.

The best response to conviction is to say, "Lord, You're right! I'm so sorry. I didn't realize how bad my attitude was. I didn't realize my words were wounding the people I love. I didn't mean to misrepresent You to people who don't know You. Will You forgive me?" In those moments, the Holy Spirit will draw you close to the Father, because that was His goal all along. He promises that if we confess our sins, He is faithful and just to forgive them (1 John 1:9). He always wants to restore fellowship.

Your guilt-suppressing and guilt-pacifying remedies aren't needed anymore. You don't need to push your mistakes down where no one, including yourself, can see them. You don't need to cover them with a few shots, purchases, or overtime hours. None of those things will relieve you of seeing yourself in the mirror. But in Christ, you can face yourself with grace and peace, because God has removed your guilt and restored your relationship with Him.

Many people, even Christians, eventually lose their moral compass. Their conscience becomes seared. The little antennas that God gives us to help us recognize right and wrong become bent and unreceptive. That's why many Christians can no longer feel guilt, even when they are living in disobedience to God. As a result, they experience destruction in their lives and relationships, and it breaks God's heart. When we confess our sins to God and let Him deal with our guilt, receiving His forgiveness and believing that there is no condemnation for those who are in Christ, the weight lifts.

Embracing the Beauty of God's Re-creation

The really exciting part of this whole process is what our freedom and restoration do within us. God makes us a new creation, as if He were speaking another genesis into being. This new life we receive by grace ushers us into discovering our unique purpose: "We are God's handiwork, created in Christ Jesus to do good works, which God prepared in advance for us to do" (Ephesians 2:10).

We have been saved by grace for a larger purpose: We are His handiwork, His workmanship, His masterpiece that shows off who He is and what He can do. He has equipped us with His own nature, which means we can walk in the kind of good works that Jesus did and that God has prepared in advance for us. He has positioned all kinds of opportunities in our future for us to express His goodness to others.

Notice the word "handiwork." Some translations say "workmanship" or "masterpiece." We get our word *poem* from this term, and it carries connotations of artistry, like the work of a potter or sculptor. God is making something magnificent out of us. We are a tapestry of grace in which all the scars and blemishes are removed, hidden on the back side, or positioned in such a way as to highlight their beauty. So we are not only *chosen, wanted, loved, secure, valuable,* and *competent,* we are *beautiful* in His eyes.

He is thoroughly delighted in who you are as His child.

Imagine God saying, "I created you from the foundation of the world, just the way you are, and even though you disobeyed and were separated from me, I have rescued you. I authored you like a profound poem, a beautiful work of art. I see your inner qualities through the lens of My Son, Jesus, and you are captivating. You're like a tapestry that is being woven with a lot of knots and tangles on the back side but with amazing colors and shapes on the front. All I notice now is the beauty that is emerging from your life."

This is how God wants you to see your life. This isn't pop psychology or positive self-talk: *You are God's masterpiece.*

You are uniquely gifted and beautiful in your inward character and outward appearance in His eyes. He is thoroughly delighted in who you are as His child.

How to See Yourself as God Sees You

Sounds too good to be true, right? Well, it's not, but it may take some hard work on your part to change the glasses you look through. In order to see yourself this way—and to be honest, not many people do—you'll need once again to replace your warped mirrors with the truth of God's Word. Some of the common misbeliefs related to guilt look like this:

Misbelief

- I am a bad person. My past mistakes and guilty feelings confirm I am dirty, ugly, and unlovable.

- If only I could be as beautiful, talented, and morally pure as _____, then I would be happy.

These are perhaps the top two lies we believe about our guilt. I'm always shocked by how many people think this way about themselves. Not *I'm a good person in God's eyes who does some occasional bad things,* but *I'm a bad person. I feel ugly. I feel unlovable.* Unfortunately, that's a belief the church has historically instilled in people by overemphasizing biblical passages about our desperately wicked hearts and our complete sinfulness.

While those things are true with regard to our fallen condition, they completely ignore the equally biblical fact that God has given us a new heart. The result is that many Christians never quite get past the thought that they are irredeemable sinners, even when they are redeemed. Those feelings are reinforced on the experiential side by tragic circumstances of emotional, physical, and/or sexual abuse that leave victims feeling guilty and ugly for years, in spite of the fact that the abuse was not their fault. It's a lie. Your true self as God defines you is beautiful, regardless of your past.

The second lie involves comparison with other people: *If only I could be like so-and-so, I would be happy.* This is an idealized picture of someone else's life, and very often that person is carrying similar pain and guilt without showing it on the outside. The truth is that if we did look, act, perform, earn income, play the piano, become a star like that person obtain whatever enviable thing that characterizes them, we would still feel dirty, ugly, unworthy, or guilty. "If only" is just another lie.

If you read enough biographies, you eventually realize how many successful people are driven by their pain. Some of the world's most successful artists, athletes, businesspeople, politicians, and academics have achieved what they have as compensation for their wounds and losses. The testimonies of people who achieved their greatest dreams—stardom, political office, a Super Bowl or World Series championship, an Olympic medal, a Nobel Prize—and remain emotionally and spiritually unfulfilled are plentiful. The perfect life we see in other people is an illusion.

What truth replaces these lies?

> ### Truth
>
> My soul (my true self), my physical appearance, my natural talents, and my personality (in their unchanging aspeots) are beautiful in God's sight. He is my Designer and Maker.

We can improve a lot of things, of course. There is always room to grow. But it won't change how God sees us. Our personalities have strengths and weaknesses, but in their unchanging aspects, they are beautiful in God's sight. He is our Designer and Maker. That's what it means to be His handiwork or workmanship, created in Christ Jesus to do good works. We are who He intended us to be. If you ever need to be reminded of that, read Psalm 139:13–17:

> For you created my inmost being;
>   you knit me together in my mother's womb.
> I praise you because I am fearfully and wonderfully
>   made;
>   your works are wonderful,
>   I know that full well.
> My frame was not hidden from you
>   when I was made in the secret place,
>   when I was woven together in the depths of the
>   earth.
> Your eyes saw my unformed body;
>   all the days ordained for me were written in your
>   book
>   before one of them came to be.

> How precious to me are your thoughts, God!
> How vast is the sum of them!

This is a journey, my friend. These truths apply to you too. You don't have to live a guilt-ridden life, because in Christ you're no longer guilty.

Questions for Reflection and Discussion

1) How have you seen guilt manifest itself in culture, in those around you, in your family, or in you?

2) What is the difference between true guilt and false guilt? Read what Paul says about our former condition in Ephesians 2:1–3. Then God intervened and out of His great love for us, He made a way to remove *all* guilt—legally, authentically, permanently. Continue reading verses 4–7. What was His solution for guilt? What was God's motive and purpose?

3) True restoration can only begin when we recognize the full extent of our need for Jesus. Have you come to the point where you realize that you can't do this yourself? Spend some time reflecting on your deep need for Jesus. Tell Jesus why you need Him.

4) What is the difference between condemnation and conviction? Who is the author of condemnation, and who is the author of conviction? What is the purpose of condemnation, and what is the purpose of conviction?

5) How do you identify and respond to condemning thoughts? How do you identify and respond to conviction? Pray and ask God for His wisdom and help in identifying and responding to condemnation as well as conviction.

6) According to Ephesians 2:10, you are God's handiwork, His masterpiece, His magnificent artwork. Close your eyes and imagine you are climbing into God's lap or

taking a walk with Him. Hear Him as He speaks to your heart these words: "You are chosen, wanted, loved, secure, valuable, uniquely gifted, competent, and beautiful in My eyes. You are My child."

Encouragement from My Journal

I understand how theoretical or abstract these thoughts about our new identity in Christ can seem sometimes, especially the more familiar with the Bible we become. I want to share with you something I wrote in my journal recently after studying this passage in Ephesians, and I hope it will be encouraging to you.

Jesus, I confess that so very often I think and emote and ponder all of these passages like some theoretical truth or mathematical equation, that You died for my sin and in my place. You rose from the grave. You conquered death, sin, and Satan. And now, what is true of You is true of me. And by faith, I have put my trust in Your work on the cross and Your resurrection.

Indeed, all that is 100 percent true, but the reality is that correct doctrine doesn't reach into the depth of my heart and being and emotions until I grasp You afresh—the fully human man with human pain, grief and exhaustion and anguish. You are not God the Force. You are God the Person.

You voluntarily suffered excruciating pain, nearly an emotional break-down, relational betrayal, desertion by Your closest friends, and worst of all, rejection by Your Father. In that moment, You allowed all my sin and the sins of everyone else to be placed on You, and the anger of the Father was justly directed against evil—not just the principle or the philosophy, but real evil in each one of us. You did all that to bring Chip Ingram, one human being—made in Your image, fallen, insecure, fearful, guilty, and completely unworthy--into a safe, secure, eternal relationship of incomprehensible love and acceptance, filled now with purpose and power and gifts. And to think that my older brother, the Lord Jesus, says without any shame, *He's My friend.*

I confess I so often fail to grasp this new life and the reality of this process, but, even when I begin to even get a faint glimpse, overwhelming gratitude is birthed in me again and I have a compelling desire to obey You and to honor You because of Your love, not because of my guilt. I want to love others more and more and treat them the way You do, regardless of how they look or what they have done or what they believe.

Please enlighten me further, that the eyes of my heart might know You better and better and better as You are, and, as a result, that I might see myself more and more as You see me. Amen.

PART 6

CALLED

11

The Lie of Angst

Early in my Christian life, I remember thinking that spiritual warfare was primarily about exorcisms, bizarre happenings, and the stuff of scary movies. I knew Jesus spoke often about Satan and confronted demons in His earthly ministry, and that the Bible taught that we're in a war and need to put on spiritual armor. But as a young Christian, my only real experience with any overt evil presence was on missions trips in developing countries. Little did I know that the great majority of all spiritual warfare occurs in the battleground of our minds.

Paul makes this very point to the Corinthians.

> Though we walk in the flesh, we do not war according to the flesh, for the weapons of our warfare are not of the flesh, but divinely powerful for the destruction of fortresses. We are destroying speculations and every lofty thing raised up against the knowledge of God, and we are taking every

thought captive to the obedience of Christ. (2 Corinthians 10:3–5 NASB)

Satan is the father of lies (John 8:44). When we have deep-seated misbeliefs about God and ourselves, there is no need for overt demonic attack.

This book is structured around six lies that have become strongholds for many of us. Each is followed by a chapter that pulls down that stronghold by helping us clearly see the truth about ourselves once we are in Christ. The misbelief/truth cards are a practical way to take every thought captive to the obedience of Christ. Reading this book will certainly be helpful, but lasting change will come in reviewing those cards, praying over them, and asking God to help you believe in your heart what you're learning.

In this chapter, I'm going to change the order and share two of the most powerful lies of the enemy. I want to address them up front because they can create dangerous emotions that have devastating consequences. These are perhaps the deepest misbeliefs that Theresa and I have had to overcome.

Misbelief

- I am not wanted or needed by anyone, my life has no purpose or meaning. I'm a victim of an unfair, uncaring world that only brings me pain.

- Significance and meaning come from success in life. I will be happy someday when my relationships, career, and finances reflect my success and accomplishments.

Truth

My life has an eternal purpose to fulfill. I have been created, equipped, and called by God in this moment of history to fulfill a unique role in His body that will demonstrate His mercy, love, diversity, and unity to the world.

"For we are His workmanship, created in Christ Jesus for good works, which God prepared beforehand so that we would walk in them."
Ephesians 2:10 (NASB)

The first misbelief is that you are not wanted or needed by anyone, that your life has no purpose or meaning, that you're a victim of an unfair, uncaring world that brings you pain. Theresa believed this with all her heart before I met her. As I shared earlier, she came from a very difficult home, was abandoned by her unbelieving husband who ran off with another woman, and was left with twin babies, no money, and a broken heart. She had a lot of reasons to believe that lie. She wrestled with some really dangerous thoughts and feelings. If not for her two children, she might not have chosen to stay in this world. She felt absolutely hopeless.

The second misbelief that held me prisoner is that significance and meaning come from success in life—that you can only be happy when your relationships, career, and finances reflect your accomplishments. Year after year of effort that produces year after year of disappointment eventually results in hopelessness. It becomes clear that this misbelief is a lie.

In my case, my upbringing actually helped in some important ways, but it also set me up for disillusionment. My Marine father and my own workaholic tendencies made me a goal setter, and I had some clear, written goals at a very early age. As I finished sixth grade, I was committed to getting a basketball scholarship, making great grades, dating a beautiful girl, and graduating among the top in my class. I did all of that.

At a party on the night of high school graduation, a friend turned to me and said something I'll never forget. She listed what I had accomplished and commented on my cute girlfriend. Then she said, "You must be very happy." And because I had already come up with a new set of goals without even enjoying the ones I had accomplished, I had a very unusual sensation: a wave of emptiness. I realized I wasn't happy at all.

Over the previous years, I had drifted away from church and had questioned whether God was real. I'd bought the lie that success will make you happy. I hadn't thought much about God or spiritual issues, but I was questioning the meaning of life. That night, while looking up at all the stars, I prayed a life-changing prayer: "God, if You exist, You better reveal Yourself to me because life makes no sense. Why am I even living? Life is meaningless. People I love will die before I do, and if accomplishing things doesn't bring meaning and happiness, it's all just a crapshoot." I challenged God to show Himself to me in a way I could understand. And if He did, I committed to follow whatever He had planned for me.

Dealing with Dangerous Emotions

Chris came from a long line of depressed people. Whether that legacy was the product of genes and brain chemistry or dysfunctional relational and thought patterns passed down from generation to generation isn't clear. It was probably the result of both nature and nurture, a mixture of physical and psychological causes.

In any case, Chris was raised in a time of turmoil, when Vietnam and civil rights and all kinds of violence and protests fueled a steady stream of TV news and daily conversation. He went to a very secular private school that was great for exposing him to a range of diverse views but also for marginalizing his own beliefs and making him ashamed of them. So early on, he began to question and doubt. By the time he was thirteen, he was a practical existentialist—as much as a thirteen-year-old can be. He still believed in God, at least theoretically and at a distance, but had no conviction that God was actually involved in his life.

Chris assumed that life had no meaning, that it's up to human beings to make meaning for themselves, and that doing so is like climbing up a steep hill or swimming against the undertow. After all, if all our meaning is fabricated in our own minds, we'll always be confronted with convincing evidence that there really is no point in making the effort. We keep slipping back into skepticism, cynicism, pessimism, and despair.

When thoughts like those take root in us, they can produce some physiological changes, such as lethargy, fatigue, and sickness. They also produce sociological changes, like alienation, antisocial behavior, feelings of inferiority, and loneliness. This downward spiral of physical and social changes fuels psychological effects too—putting a person in a terrible, dark, and dangerous place.

At times, Chris felt almost nothing, as if he were already dead inside. He began to come out of this vicious cycle a few years later when he hit the bottom and pleaded with God either to make his life better or go ahead and end it. Providentially, God reconnected him with some Christian friends who made an extra effort to bring him out of his isolation and demonstrate real fellowship and love.

That may have saved Chris's life, but it didn't completely end his struggles. The effects of depression and despair can linger quite a while: our brain chemistry, neurological pathways, and behavioral patterns don't change overnight. Chris was treated for depression twice as an adult. He describes those seasons as a perpetual drizzly, foggy day, or as he puts it, "Always Seattle in my soul."

But over time, Chris learned to see life and himself differently, and he began to feel a consistent and ever-increasing sense of hope. He found a true sense of calling and purpose. Today, many years later, he has come so far that he has a strong aversion to negative attitudes and faithless words, and he lives in anticipation of God's best.

But for a time, before he encountered the truth of God's Word and let it sink into his heart—a long process, to be sure—he was a high-risk teenager and a moody young adult. As with Theresa and me in those earlier years, some pretty scary thoughts were running free in his mind. He was steeped in a dangerous way of thinking, feeling, and responding to the world around him.

Unfortunately, stories like Chris's aren't unusual. In fact, we're living in a day of an epidemic rise in depression and suicide among teens and those in midlife.

How Do You Deal with Angst?

So, let me ask you, how do you handle hopelessness, frustration, or times when you sense that life is meaningless? Or thoughts that you might as well not live anymore?

I'm not sure how to categorize all of those feelings, but I think *angst* captures most of them. Angst is a feeling of deep anxiety and dread that is unfocused and hard to identify. It's a sense of frustration and apprehension with the general state of the world and one's future in it. And it's often accompanied by depression. That sums up Theresa's hopelessness when she was abandoned by her first husband; it sums up my emptiness after realizing my accomplishments didn't make me happy, and it sums up Chris's despair. In fact, it sums up a lot of people's approach to life.

Angst, hopelessness, anxiety, and this whole package of emotions may be hard to identify, but they're not hard to understand. Just look at the headlines. Look at the state of people's relationships. Maybe look inside. We see a lot of terrible things happening in the world that, if you didn't know better, might cause you to think life is meaningless. And you begin to wonder: *What about me? Am I meaningless too?* It isn't difficult to get discouraged or depressed. Our world and our past experiences war against our own happiness and fulfillment.

Angst has some emotional cousins. One of them is a recurring thought of meaninglessness. Sometimes this is not a conscious thought; it's just a sense, a mood, a lack of interest in or energy about life and its direction. It feels like your life has no value or significance or purpose—like no one would miss you if you were gone. That's where Theresa was for a season, and it was incredibly painful.

Another emotional cousin of angst is *purposelessness*—living without aim, a goal, or a plan. Life feels pointless and senseless, with no discernible direction to it or even any way to create one. That was where I was after realizing my plans didn't produce the satisfaction I thought they would. What's the point? Why keep going? Why bother if nothing leads to happiness?

This package of emotions—or, for many people, emotionlessness—tends to produce hopelessness, another cousin of angst. It's a belief that nothing good can happen and a happy ending is either impossible or very unlikely. It's despair, despondence, a conviction or nagging feeling that things will never get better. Real change, a happier day, is always out there but ever elusive, never really coming.

And when you lose hope, horrible things happen. Suicide has skyrocketed in the last decade. A secular study investigating the causes asked whether it was education, lack of emotional support of family and friends, or some other reason people were killing themselves in record numbers. Do you know what they found? The clearest cause they could identify was a combination of a lack of religion, no sense of meaning, and the decline of a coherent worldview and the belief that there is a God and a larger purpose that gives life meaning.[1]

Unhealthy Responses to Angst

Angst is real, and it isn't only about suicide. I believe most people experience angst at some point in their lives. We go through dips of discouragement and depression, and even the most good-natured and positive people still ask the big questions that bring moments of angst.

That's one of the reasons I love to read the Psalms. David was a man after God's own heart, yet he could be dancing before the Lord in worship one day and in a valley asking why God had forsaken him the next. He even asked God to take his life if that's what God wanted. He was a faith-filled person, and yet some of his writings make him sound clinically depressed. So this may not be just somebody else's problem. It may be yours or a friend's or a family member's. It is a common human experience.

Angst provokes some pretty unhealthy responses. People feeling hopelessness, purposelessness, or meaninglessness tend to withdraw from other people, develop addictive behaviors or relationships, act out, cultivate a victim mentality, engage in trivial pursuits as a way of searching for some meaning or masking its absence, and in worst-case scenarios, commit suicide. It isn't easy to be friends with someone who is depressed or filled with anxiety, and the relational distance that results only makes the problem worse. The emotions and emotionlessness that come with angst and its cousins are extremely hard to deal with and cause us to worry about friends who are wrestling with them.

> *Angst provokes some pretty unhealthy responses.*

How Do You Deal with Dangerous Emotions?

Apart from Jesus, what do you use to soothe or sedate your sense of angst? How do you respond when you feel like life is senseless? What do you do when you feel discouraged and depressed? How do you handle hopelessness?

Do you try to cover it by working more, eating more, shopping more, medicating yourself more, drinking more, or having more sex? Or do you withdraw, numb your feelings, deny your desires, lose your energy, and wish you could crawl into a hole and die?

As with so many of these attitudes and distortions of our true selves, responses tend to go in one of two directions: compulsion or withdrawal. But each of those can take many forms. If you have any experience with the emotions or at-titudes related to angst, which tend to characterize you?

I've seen people show up at church and immediately realize they can relate to a message like this. Sometimes they want to engage right away and get involved in a group. They think, *If there's help for this, I want it.* That's great, and I hope that's true of you if this is something you struggle with.

But one of the greatest problems with hopelessness and de-pression is the sense that nothing will help; that even if some-thing looks like it might help, it probably isn't worth trying. This set of emotions has a paralyzing effect at a time when people most need to get up and do something. Whatever you do, don't let it paralyze you. If you'll take a step toward God, He will take every other step toward you, no matter how many it takes. But you have to respond.

Here's the deal: We all have issues, and this is a really com-mon one, but if you'll identify your angst and muster up the courage to address it, God will meet you there. It isn't easy, and if you need help, by all means ask for it. If dangerous thoughts are running through your mind, talk with your pastor, a counselor, a family member, or a friend. But please do something. If you're willing to be honest, even privately with God, the antidote to angst will make a lot of sense.

God has a solution for our feelings of meaninglessness and purposelessness, and I'll share that with you in the next chap-ter. It's what turned Chris's, Theresa's, and my lives around, and God wants the same for you.

Questions for Reflection and Discussion

1) Has there ever been a time in your life when you felt unwanted or that life had no purpose? Perhaps you've felt that life is just an unfair, uncaring, hopeless string of events of which people are victims. Describe.

2) What does the "American Dream" advertise about happiness? Have you acquired the relationship, the acclaim, the car, the job, and the house, only to find that you are not happy?

3) Angst is real. Chris described the feelings of living with angst as "Always Seattle in my soul." Have you experienced a season of angst or one of its emotional cousins: meaninglessness, purposelessness, emotionlessness, or hopelessness? Perhaps you are in a season like that now. Which of the emotional cousins do you most identify with?

4) David was a man after God's own heart, and he shared his emotional turmoil throughout the Psalms. Take a moment to read and reflect on this psalm:

> As the deer pants for the water brooks,
> So my soul pants for You, O God.
> My soul thirsts for God, for the living God;
> When shall I come and appear before God?
> My tears have been my food day and night,
> While they say to me all day long, "Where is your God?"
> These things I remember and I pour out my soul within me.
> For I used to go along with the throng and lead them in
>   procession to the house of God,

With the voice of joy and thanksgiving, a multitude keeping festival.

Why are you in despair, O my soul?
And why have you become disturbed within me?
Hope in God, for I shall again praise Him
For the help of His presence.
O my God, my soul is in despair within me;
Therefore I remember You from the land of the Jordan
And the peaks of Hermon, from Mount Mizar.
Deep calls to deep at the sound of Your waterfalls;
All Your breakers and Your waves have rolled over me.
The Lord will command His lovingkindness in the
daytime;
And His song will be with me in the night,
A prayer to the God of my life.

I will say to God my rock, "Why have You forgotten me?
Why do I go mourning because of the oppression of the
enemy?"
As a shattering of my bones, my adversaries revile me,
While they say to me all day long, "Where is your God?"
Why are you in despair, O my soul?
And why have you become disturbed within me?
Hope in God, for I shall yet praise Him,
The help of my countenance and my God.
(Psalm 42:1–11 NASB)

What stands out to you in this psalm? What emotions does David experience? How does he cope with
them? What brings David hope?

5) How do you cope with your emotions?

12

You Are Called

Ephesians 2:11–3:21

When my friend Connie walks into a room, immediately there's an energy, a contagious smile, an emotional warmth, and a passion that flows from her. There's something about her life, attitude, and demeanor that's positive and encouraging.

But Connie's life wasn't always like this. She's had her share of angst, hopelessness, discouragement, and purposelessness. Connie's marriage didn't survive the fast-paced, Silicon Valley high-tech position that she held. Her soul didn't survive the corporate success and accolades that failed to deliver the peace and satisfaction she longed for. Connie was a follower of Christ, but like many of us, she was held captive by strongholds and lies about herself, about God, and about her future.

In 2008, Connie was prompted to get her focus off herself and follow a nudge from the Holy Spirit. With no money, no staff, and no location, she set out to help disadvantaged kids hear about the love of Jesus and give them a shot at a better life by providing some educational opportunities that were currently out of their reach.

She started a camp called SAM—Science, Art, and Math—in these neighborhoods. She recruited friends and volunteers to go in for a week, teach science, art, and math, and talk about God's love. She doesn't charge very much for the camp, and she never turns anyone away. Hundreds of kids come and have the experience of a lifetime. They learn a lot and, often for the first time, are exposed to God's Word.

Connie gets super excited when she talks about this camp. Her heart leaps with joy because she knew this was what God wanted her to do. As she learned how God had gifted her and was open to do whatever He desired, she realized how her desires were converging with God's to accomplish His purposes—Connie calls it her calling. She now lives with a deep sense of satisfaction and purpose as she sees lives change and shares stories of how God has given hope and meaning to kids, parents, and volunteers. Her angst has been swallowed up as she experiences God's approval and witnesses the miracles in the lives of children that no one else cared about.

God's Antidotes to Angst

Much of what Paul has written in the first two chapters of Ephesians that we have covered directly addresses the emotional turmoil of hopelessness. Knowing who we are created to be and what God has given us in salvation goes a long way toward relieving our feelings of angst. Connie's journey wasn't magical, and neither is yours or mine. We are called into a new relationship, a new family, and a new purpose for our lives. How do we discover our calling?

First, remember the hope of your calling. We've seen in Ephesians 1 that we are *chosen* because we are accepted, *adopted* because we are wanted, *redeemed* because we are valuable, *sealed* to make us secure, and *empowered* to make us competent. In verse 17, Paul prayed that God would give the Ephesians a spirit of wisdom and revelation for a true, intimate, experiential knowledge of Him. In the next verse, he prayed that they would also know the hope of His calling. Paul wanted his readers to grasp the love of their Father, how infinitely valuable they were, and how securely they could live in Him. At a foundational level, that's what it means to be called. Everything God sees when He looks at us is true. When we ponder these truths, it changes the way we live.

> *Knowing who we are created to be and what God has given us in salvation goes a long way toward relieving our feelings of angst.*

Call is one of those words the Bible associates with our salvation. The words for *call* in both Hebrew and Greek can be used in the sense of naming or bestowing an identity (Genesis 2:19; Luke 1:13). When God bestows a name or identity upon us, He is essentially creating, just as He did when He called forth billions of stars by name (Isaiah 40:26).

He also spoke to each of us, creating us with His words. In turn, we respond in faith. This idea may seem foreign to us in the twenty-first century, but it is something God does in our salvation. He re-creates us and calls us. He gives us a new identity.

People who think their identity is in their work, appearance, family, status, money, or achievements will eventually experience disillusionment. But those who realize their highest, greatest identity is in being a beloved and secure son or daughter of the King will not be disillusioned. Just as God spoke at creation, He speaks at our re-creation to make us new. The old things have passed away. We can only experience that as we exercise faith and remember the hope of His calling.

People who think their identity is in their work, appearance, family, status, money, or achievements will eventually experience disillusionment.

Second, reflect on the magnitude of your calling. This is where Paul takes us next in Ephesians 2:11–3:21. He is trying to help us grasp the ungraspable. When our eyes catch a glimpse of what God has done for us, all those issues that seem to keep us trapped and helpless begin to dissipate, and all those efforts we make to cover them or compensate for them aren't relevant anymore.

In the first three chapters of Ephesians, Paul gives us five specific ways God called us. The first two are a review of what we have already seen; the others build on that foundation.

Together, they paint a picture of the magnitude of God's calling.

1. *God calls us into a new relationship (Ephesians 1:3–4).* We have been chosen in Christ before the foundation of the world to be holy and blameless in His sight. We were not called to be religious, to follow a moral code, to fulfill a duty, or to come under the burden of a list of things we're supposed to do or not supposed to do. We were called into a relationship with Jesus.

In John 15, on the night before His crucifixion, Jesus was talking to His disciples in a vineyard, preparing them for what would soon come: "I no longer call you servants," He told them, "because a servant does not know his master's business. Instead, I have called you friends, for everything that I learned from my Father I have made known to you" (v. 15). Did you notice the shift in the relationship? According to Jesus's words, you're His friend. God has called you into a close relationship, not a guilt-ridden duty.

2. *God calls us into a new purpose (Ephesians 2:10).* As we saw in this verse in Ephesians, we are the workmanship, the evidence of His artistry. That means there's never been anyone else like you on the face of the earth. Like your unique physical DNA, your spiritual DNA has the capacity to reflect God and honor Him in a way that no one else can. He created you exactly the way He wanted you to be in order to fulfill something no one else can. You are not a last-minute idea, an afterthought, or an improvisation. He knew you before the foundation of the world and prepared for your relationship with Him. Your purpose was carefully chosen.

211

There are two sides to that purpose—a general one and a specific one. Your general calling is similar to everyone else's, even though you will carry it out in unique ways, with your own personality and mix of spiritual gifts, talents, and skills. Like everyone, you are called to love God and love others, to do good works, to glorify God and bear fruit in His kingdom. That fruit is, in large part, your character. As you allow Jesus to live His life in and through you, you become kinder, more loving, more patient, less envious, less arrogant, and more generous. You begin to think, talk, and act more and more like Jesus. That's the Father's goal—for us to become like Him, each with a unique expression of His nature that fits our personality but is conformed to Jesus in character. You are, in Jesus's words, "the light of the world." He told us to let our light shine before others so they see our good works and glorify God (Matthew 5:16).

But God also has a specific purpose for us, good works that are uniquely designed for us. Imagine the worldwide church, the body of Christ across the earth, as a huge puzzle with you as one of its pieces. No matter how minor you may think your role is, the picture isn't complete without you. No one else can bring the same package of personality, gifts, desires, testimonies, and opportunities. You fit in such a manner as to help people see God in a way they can't see Him through anyone else.

I call this specific calling a *holy ambition*. Sometimes it takes some time to figure out what it is, but we all have one within us—a dream of serving God in a particular way that fulfills our God-given purpose. Theologian Frederick Buechner writes, "The place God calls you to is the place where your deep gladness and the world's deep hunger meet."[1] A holy ambition takes us there—to the intersection of our unique capacity to serve and the world's need for what we bring.

Connie's holy ambition is leveraging her career in technology and business to give kids practical knowledge and spiritual insight. Mine is teaching God's Word in a way that provokes real life change. I've done that through teaching series and books like this one, in pulpits and on the radio, and any other way I can think of. One of the ways we've done that at Living on the Edge is by creating three- or four-minute videos to use as family devotionals. They are aimed at kids, and each one highlights an attribute of God. When I hear that a child has asked their mom or dad if they can

> *A holy ambition takes us to the intersection of our unique capacity to serve and the world's need for what we bring.*

watch another one, then another one, and another, that satisfies my sense of purpose in a way that's hard to describe. When we see God move through the good works and acts of service we offer to Him, meaninglessness is no longer an issue.

Whatever you think will make you happy will ultimately prove unsatisfying unless it involves discovering your unique purpose and giving your life to it. The Spirit of God will inspire and energize your ordinary efforts to produce something that will change people for eternity. No drug or habit can do that.

A young woman came up to me between services one Sunday. She told me she had traveled up from San Diego just to go to church. She credited something in my messages with changing her life and saving her marriage and family. I know that's entirely the work of the Holy Spirit, and that He touches lives in many ways through many ministries all the time, but as I listened to her story and saw the tears in her eyes, I was overwhelmed to be a part of it. Joy and gratification filled my heart in a way that's hard to express. Our workaholism is unnecessary when God is at work, because He can accomplish so much in such little time. Our holy ambition becomes His means for reaching the world through the power of His Spirit.

> *No achievement, stock portfolio, or second home can compare with experiencing the meaning and purpose of our calling.*

No achievement, stock portfolio, or second home can compare with experiencing the meaning and purpose of our calling. God brought us into a new relationship with Jesus and gave us both a general and specific calling to fulfill our purpose. Pursue that and discover it, and angst melts away.

3. God calls us into a new family (Ephesians 2:11–22). Now we venture into new territory in Ephesians 2. Verses 11–22 describe a new family, and we need a bit of context for this. Paul is writing to a largely Gentile church that's still learning about the Jewish background of their faith. Jesus was a Jew, of course, and fulfilled Old Testament prophecies as the Jewish Messiah. Paul essentially tells these Gentile believers that they need to remember where they came from. They were formerly hostile to God and alienated from Him, without hope and without access to God's promises (vv. 11–13). They were on the outside looking in. But Paul then turns to Jewish believers, who could at times act more than a little exclusive, and reminds them that Jesus broke down the dividing wall between Jews and Gentiles (vv. 14–18). The words "peace" and "unity" come up often in this passage because Paul is emphasizing the new creation as an entirely new entity.

This sets the stage for Paul's key point:

> Consequently, you are no longer foreigners and strangers, but fellow citizens with God's people and also members of his household, built on the foundation of the apostles and prophets, with Christ Jesus himself as the chief cornerstone. In him the whole building is joined together and rises to become a holy temple in the Lord. And in him you too are being built together to become a dwelling in which God lives by his Spirit. (vv. 19–22)

Why do people go to temples? To worship, to experience God's presence, to participate in a community of faith. God has created one new family out of Jews and Gentiles, a new creation that He inhabits Himself. God's presence dwells in each believer individually, but that presence multiplies and manifests when we come together. He's built us together as a temple in order to manifest His presence to us and through us for our own sake and for the sake of the world.

Few of us understand the tension that existed between Jews and Gentiles at the time this was written. They looked down on each other. Most Gentiles thought Jews were a strange ethnic group, and many Jews thought Gentiles were unclean dogs.

Paul is saying that in Jesus, these animosities and divisions have been removed. There's unity in Christ. No believer is born of a Gentile Spirit or a Jewish Spirit; there's only one Holy Spirit, and He has birthed all who come to Christ in faith. A modern-day equivalent might be something like the KKK and the NAACP joining hands to work together, or Hamas and the Israeli government deciding they can get along. That's how radical this unity is meant to be. In Jesus, we're members of the same family no matter what biases we once held.

We tend to hang out with people we like. Even in Christian circles, believers tend to gravitate toward people who are similar to us. We like to be with people who speak our language, either literally or figuratively. I know there are plenty of exceptions; in recent years, church fellowships have grown much more diverse than they used to be. But being in the same room with people from different backgrounds and getting to know them through strong social and emotional bonds are two different things. The fellowship in the family of God is meant to go deep and cross all those boundaries.

Imagine yourself being in Ephesus and reading Paul's letter. Think of the diversity around you in the city—the extremely rich and the enslaved, the soldiers and the revolutionaries, the different ethnic and religious backgrounds. How does a motley group of people who would normally ignore or even hate each other now join together in the same family? Those are the kinds of divisions we are called to bridge in Christ.

This is not just a question for Paul's time. We certainly have our modern equivalents of groups that don't associate with each other. But there are churches where diverse people raise their hands together in worship and hold hands to pray. And if we really understood what God has done to break down these walls, that would happen a lot more. We live in a day where our identity must be rooted first and foremost in Christ; not in race, political party, denomination, or socioeconomics.

The point is that we are called not just to accomplish something but to be part of a new creation, a new family.

The early Church transformed a fractured and violent world, because people with radical differences began to grasp in their heads and hearts what it meant to be in this new family. Like the early Church, we must pull down strongholds and replace them with truths like this: *I am secure and loved. I have all I need in Jesus and give my life away to Him and, through Him, to others. As I give my life away, God multiplies my effort and gives me far more than I gave. The more I am willing to serve, make connections, and live full of grace, the more God does through me. My life has purpose and meaning as a member of His family and part of His eternal plan.*

> *Like the early church, we must pull down strongholds and replace them with truths.*

4. *God calls us to fulfill His new plan (Ephesians 3:1–13).* God has called us into a new relationship with Him, a new purpose in His kingdom, and a new family with His people. He also calls us into a new plan. Three times in the first six verses of chapter 3, Paul uses the word "mystery." The Greek word does not mean something that cannot be explained and remains shrouded in uncertainty but, instead, means something that was once hidden, a secret.

But Paul is also clear that this mystery is no longer secret (v. 5). "This mystery is that through the gospel the Gentiles are heirs together with Israel, members together of one body, and sharers together in the promise in Christ Jesus" (v. 6). The church is made up of Jews and Gentiles, rich and poor, slaves and free, male and female—everyone who believes in Jesus. All become one new family, and this family has an agenda.

> His intent was that now, through the church, the manifold wisdom of God should be made known to the rulers and authorities in the heavenly realms, according to his eternal purpose that he accomplished in Christ Jesus our Lord. In him and through faith in him we may approach God with freedom and confidence. I ask you, therefore, not to be discouraged because of my sufferings for you, which are your glory. (vv. 10–13)

God's agent of blessing was Israel, but the Jewish people were only the beginning of the plan, not the end. In bringing together diverse people in Christ, God created a new entity we now call the Church.

Through the Church, according to verse 10, He wants to make His wisdom known to all spiritual beings in heavenly realms, to the rulers and authorities, to principalities and powers, to all of creation seen and unseen by human eyes. Angels in heaven have worshiped God and covered their eyes because of His holiness. They are astounded that fallen human beings who were once dead in their sins—angry and envious, and seemingly irreconcilable to both God and each other—are now united together in one body of love and grace.

Part of our calling as believers is to demonstrate grace, to educate heavenly beings in the ways of God, to give them access to a side of God they have never seen, so that His manifold, infinite wisdom and grace might become visible. We are called to be evidence of what God's heart is like. And this, according to verse 11, was according to God's eternal purpose which He accomplished in Jesus.

You, then, are part of an eternal plan and have a unique role in it. Your role is to give away your life—a life like no one else's—to go into the world and make disciples and to simply live each day as a reflection of God's grace. That's what Jesus was getting at in the Great Commission (Matthew 28:18–20) when He told His followers not simply to educate everyone about what the Bible says but to teach people to live the truth. And that purpose comes with a promise that He will empower us and never leave us alone.

When you grasp this amazing calling God has given you, it's hard to be discouraged and depressed, isn't it? Can anyone believe they're part of these eternal purposes of God and still think life is meaningless? Life really does make sense. It does have direction. We're called to be God's friends. We have a new relationship, a new purpose, a new family, and a new plan. Each one of us is the only person who can fulfill our particular role in this plan, because each individual is uniquely designed to fit in God's big puzzle. We get to be part of something big and everlasting. That's life changing.

We live in a world that is navel gazing, obsessed with its own fulfillment, and full of narcissistic impulses—a consumer society that picks and chooses what it wants and rejects what it doesn't. That attitude has even crept into churches, where people complain when the music goes a little long, the message doesn't make them feel good, the people are too weird or hypocritical or awkward, and so on. But the church doesn't exist for the consumer. It exists for God. The music, the message, and the members are all ultimately for Him. We get to be a part of it. We're participants in God's eternal plan.

When you grasp this amazing calling God has given you, it's hard to be discouraged and depressed.

God's calling is so big, so amazing, and so magnificently awesome that just leaning into it and experiencing it will radically change the course of our lives. Even the secular world realizes that life is more than making money and achieving impressive things. Throughout history, people such as the Carnegies, the Rockefellers, the Fords, and the Gateses made a lot of money but were unsatisfied until they started giving it away. Those foundations and charities they created are filling a void, because everyone—the religious and the nonreligious—understands the importance of the bigger cause.

What greater cause is there than the gospel of salvation and the mission of the kingdom of God? I want to be part of that, and I can't imagine who wouldn't, if they only knew that its great meaning and purpose and fullness never end.

5. *God calls us to make our hearts Christ's home (Ephesians 3:14–21)*. Paul began with our new relationship and ends this section with an amazing prayer that deepens the relationship beyond our understanding.

> For this reason I kneel before the Father, from whom every family in heaven and on earth derives its name. I pray that out of his glorious riches he may strengthen you with power through his Spirit in your inner being, so that Christ may dwell in your hearts through faith. And I pray that you, being rooted and established in love, may have power, together with all the Lord's holy people, to grasp how wide and long and high and deep is the love of Christ, and to know this love that surpasses knowledge—that you may be filled to the measure of all the fullness of God.
>
> Now to him who is able to do immeasurably more than all we ask or imagine, according to his power that is at work within us, to him be glory in the church and in Christ Jesus throughout all generations, for ever and ever! Amen. (Ephesians 3:14–21)

God's calling is so big, so amazing, and so magnificently awesome that just leaning into it and experiencing it will radically change the course of our lives.

"For this reason" points back to all that Paul has written up to this point. In light of all of these glorious truths, Paul prays his second big prayer in this letter, and it focuses on God's power at work in the depths of our being. We need His strength to take the kinds of steps He wants us to take and to walk in the power He wants us to walk in. The point, as verse 17 says, is that Christ would dwell in our hearts by faith. Our hearts should be the kind of environment in which Jesus is right at home.

Only God can transform our hearts to be in that condition. He is absolutely holy, transcendent, and awesome, but He wants to be our friend. He invites us to come boldly into His throne room, where normally we would have no right to be (Hebrews 4:16). We've been adopted into the royal family, and we can hang out with the King—with reverence, of course, but also with great familiarity. We can talk to Him when we're driving in the car or walking in the neighborhood. When we realize we've made a mistake, we can say, "Oh, Lord, I'm sorry," without having to clean ourselves up before He'll talk with us again. We can have conversations with Him about the issues of life just like we would with any other friend, except in this case our Friend can do a lot about them. If He's at home in our hearts, we can be at home with Him.

Paul prays that we would be rooted and established in love and that we would have power together with all of God's people to enter into the full experience of these truths. Everything he's described so far is impossible without the power and love of God. It isn't difficult; it's impossible. We need each other for this journey. God will sometimes answer a prayer for comfort, guidance, provision, wisdom, encouragement, and anything else we need with a direct supernatural experience, but usually He provides through other believers. That's why no single person has every spiritual gift or all the resources they need; we're designed to be interdependent and experience God through each other. That's where we encounter His love and power most often.

You'll see this dynamic again and again. Someone has a need and another believer has the means and the desire to meet it, often at exactly the right time. Someone is desperate to hear God's voice on an issue, and another believer has a conversation, preaches a message, or shares a testimony that addresses that issue clearly. That's one of the greatest benefits we receive from the challenges and crises we have already faced; they become launching pads for helping others through the same struggles. Every believer receives the ministry of God through the gifts and service of other believers around them. That's how this new family, the body of Christ, works.

> *That's one of the greatest benefits we receive from the challenges and crises we have already faced; they become launching pads for helping others through the same struggles.*

You'll find God working through you this way often if you make yourself available to Him. You may be in the middle of a conversation with someone and realize you have something to share that addresses his or her particular problem. Your friend might find it to be an amazing insight, and you'll think it was only a regular comment from a regular person. But if you are prompted by the Holy Spirit and speak in a moment of openness, it can be life changing. When He is at home in your heart, things come out of it that build His people up.

Next, Paul prays that we would know the love that surpasses knowledge—that we'd know the unknowable, that the fact of His love would become intimate knowledge—and that we'd be filled with the fullness of God. That is an astounding statement. You and I don't have the capacity to be filled with the fullness of God (even the universe can't contain Him), but we can be filled to overflowing with every aspect of His nature. If we're filled with God, we have no need to fill ourselves with superficial pleasures, entertainment, activities, or whatever we might use to soothe or stimulate our soul. God gazes into our hearts, sees the truth of who we really are, and promises to fill us with His love and even the fullness of His own nature. We have to let go of the substitutes. But when we do, He makes His presence felt.

Do you want that? Reading it, agreeing with it, and even being inspired by it are not enough. Do you want to take the next step and receive His calling? Are you willing to reflect on the magnitude of your calling and what it would take to experience it?

Four Vital Questions to Remove the Angst in Your Life

These four questions will help you take the next steps.

1. Have you responded to Jesus's calling you to Himself?

Removing angst begins with complete honesty about your need for Christ and about your own sin. It isn't difficult to say, "I am not who I need to be. Forgive me, Lord. Fill my emptiness with Yourself." It's not a long prayer but a profound one and a good request for each day.

2. Have you discovered Jesus's purpose for your life?

Connie was a Christian who was involved in a lot of different things, all of which were good, but she narrowed them down and discovered what she discerned she was made to do. You aren't called to do everything. You're called to do the good works God has prepared for you—the things that fit your gifts, passions, and opportunities. Sometimes it takes a lot of prayer and searching to find your purpose, but it's a journey God is more than happy to walk through with you.

3. Are you an active, connected member of Jesus's family?

Are you living in community with other believers? Are you regularly sharing your gifts and wisdom with them and receiving theirs? Do you have people in your life who allow you to take off your mask, who love you for you, and who will help you grow in Christ?

4. Are you actively part of God's plan to reach, teach, and serve others?

Church culture over the years has unwittingly trained people to think that being a follower of Jesus is primarily about gathering at a building on Sundays, singing some songs, listening to a message, and trying to be a nice person during the week. Those activities certainly have merit, but if that's all you pass on to your children, don't be surprised if they don't follow your religious example. The Christian life is so much more. It is a supernatural adventure that involves teaching, serving, loving, and giving our lives away. That's what Jesus did and that's how we experience it in its fullness. Otherwise, we're pieces of the puzzle that are still missing.

In a very practical sense, you are indispensable for God's ideal. Theologically speaking, that isn't entirely true; God will accomplish His ultimate purposes with or without you.

But He wants to accomplish them with you, and He has designed you to be indispensable to His body locally and as a whole. Your puzzle piece is needed for the big picture. If you ever wanted to discover a sense of significance, there it is. You're needed.

How to See Yourself as God Sees You

The warped mirrors and misbeliefs about the meaning and purpose of our lives must be replaced with God's truth. Consider these cards again:

Misbelief

- I am not wanted or needed by anyone, my life has no purpose or meaning. I'm a victim of an unfair, uncaring world that only brings me pain.

- Significance and meaning come from success in life. I will be happy someday when my relationships, career, and finances reflect my success and accomplishments.

Truth

My life has an eternal purpose to fulfill. I have been created, equipped, and called by God in this moment of history to fulfill a unique role in His body that will demonstrate His mercy, love, diversity, and unity to the world.

"For we are His workmanship, created in Christ Jesus for good works, which God prepared beforehand so that we would walk in them."
Ephesians 2:10 (NASB)

Now, read the truth card again and again, slowly and thoughtfully, hearing God as He calls your name. Ask Him to instill in you a holy ambition that you can pursue and fulfill to your great satisfaction and joy. Do whatever God calls you to do to make the greatest and deepest impact on the most people with whatever He has given you. The reward will be beyond your wildest dreams, now and forever.

Questions for Reflection and Discussion

1) What brings you joy, deep satisfaction, and a sense of purpose in life?

2) Below are God's two antidotes for angst. In your own words, write out what each antidote means.

   • *Remember the hope of your calling:*
   • *Reflect on the magnitude of your calling:*

   Is there one of the two that resonates most with you? Why?

3) In the first three chapters of Ephesians, God gives us four specific ways He has called us.

   • God calls us into a new relationship. (Ephesians 1:3–4)
   • God calls us to a new purpose. (Ephesians 2:10)
   • God calls us into a new family. (Ephesians 2:11–22)
   • God calls us to make our hearts Christ's home. (Ephesians 3:14–21)

   How might you reflect on the magnitude of your calling and what it would take to experience it?

4) These four vital questions will help you take the next steps in removing angst in your life. Reflect on each question and answer honestly.

   • Have you responded to Jesus's calling you to Himself?

- Have you discovered Jesus's purpose in your life?
- Are you an active, connected member of Jesus's family?
- Are you actively part of God's plan to reach, teach, and serve others?

5) Pray and ask God to help you hear Him and see Him at work in you. Ask for His guidance in seeing the real you and instilling in you a holy ambition. What next step is God asking you to take in order to experience your calling? Tell a trusted friend about it.

Conclusion

Your Journey Has Only Just Begun

When you entered into a relationship with Christ, it probably wasn't so your life could stay the same. Like most believers, you wanted something new. You wanted to leave your old ways behind and experience the rebirth God promises and live as a new creation. This book has been an exploration of what that means. I hope you have discovered along the way that it's possible—that the gospel really does address our deepest needs and heal our deepest wounds, even those that have been with us for years. I hope you've been encouraged to take steps to embrace every spiritual blessing God has given us in Christ.

As we close our time together, I encourage you to pray with me for each of us to experience the fullness of God's richest blessing and His purposes for our lives. Make that prayer a part of your daily conversation with God and watch how He answers over time. Be patient and persistent. Give His plans time to unfold. But fully expect to see Him at work as He weaves your gifts and desires into His purposes, for His plans and His kingdom. God is very much for you and available in your search for your true self. He has authored your true identity and He's absolutely committed to helping you find it.

In our time together, we've talked about the issues of the human heart that have been with us since time and eternity. Since the great and catastrophic fall of man, our challenges with fear, insignificance, insecurity, guilt, and shame have been with us. To experience those struggles, and to be perplexed at times or confused in your journey with those issues, only means that you're human.

But we also have a great Savior, who by His life, death, and resurrection has given us new life, has defeated the power and the penalty of sin, has conquered the works of the enemy, and has implanted in us a brand-new nature as sons and daughters of the living God. This book unpacks the meat of God's Word. As an exposition of the first three chapters of the book of Ephesians, we've covered many of the great doctrines of the church—election, redemption, inheritance, sealing of the Spirit, the depravity of man, the new birth, the sovereign plan of God for Jew and Gentile.

In my experience as a pastor for over thirty years, it seems that only serious Bible students learn these core doctrines, and they learn them for an exam or as sacred truths to be guarded, which is well and good. But they were never written or intended to be great truths just for Bible students. They're intended to be truth that all Christ followers would abide in,

understand, and begin to believe with ever-increasing measure, so our lives would actually change and become more
and more like Jesus.

I encourage you to pray with me for yourself and for others, that what's already true of us—about who we are in
Christ—might be experienced by all who call ourselves followers of Jesus.

> *Lord, will You please open our minds and enlighten our
> hearts? For those who have never crossed the line, who
> have never confessed to You that they need You, that
> they are not perfect, that they have done things wrong,
> I pray that they would ask for forgiveness, place their
> full trust in You, and enter into Your resurrection life.
> And I pray that all of us would grow each and every
> day in our understanding of what it means to be Your
> daughter or son.*
>
> *Lord, I also pray for all of us who have crossed that
> line into life that we would see ourselves the way You
> do—that each of us would know our true identity and
> live in it daily. As You call each of us by name, show us
> what it means to be chosen and adopted, significant,
> secure, competent, beautiful, and called. Show us what
> it means to be Your friends. Make Your home in our
> hearts, fill us with holy ambition, lead us into lives
> of purpose and fruitfulness, and root us in the height,
> depth, width, and breadth of Your love. Whatever we
> need to do, show us the next step.*
>
> *In Jesus's name, Amen.*

Notes

Introduction
1. A. W. Tozer, *The Knowledge of the Holy* (New York: HarperCollins, 1978), 1.

Chapter 1 The Lie of Rejection
1. Tozer, *Knowledge of the Holy*, 1.
2. Tozer, *Knowledge of the Holy*, 1.

Chapter 3 The Lie of Insignificance
1. Robert McGee, *The Search for Significance: Seeing Your True Worth Through God's Eyes* (Nashville: Thomas Nelson, 2003), 7.
2. C. S. Lewis, *Mere Christianity* (New York: HarperOne, 2017), 136.

Chapter 7 The Lie of Shame
1. Brené Brown, *Daring Greatly: How the Courage to Be Vulnerable Transforms the Way We Live, Love, Parent, and Lead* (New York: Avery, 2015), 69.
2. Rachel Simmons, *Enough As She Is: How to Help Girls Move Beyond Impossible Standards of Success to Live Healthy, Happy, and Fulfilling Lives* (New York: Harper, 2018).

Chapter 9 The Lie of Guilt
1. Becca Cowan Johnson, *Good Guilt, Bad Guilt: And What to Do with Each* (Downers Grove, IL: InterVarsity Press, 1996).

Chapter 11 The Lie of Angst
1. Ben Shapiro, "CDC: Youth Suicide Skyrockets 70% Over Last Decade. Here's Why," DailyWire.com, March 20, 2018, accessed at https://www.dailywire.com/news/28449/cdc-youth-suicide-skyrockets-70-over-last-decade-ben-shapiro.

Chapter 12 You Are Called
1. Frederick Buechner, *Wishful Thinking*, expanded ed. (New York: HarperOne, 1993).

Chip Ingram is the teaching pastor and CEO of Living on the Edge, an international teaching and discipleship ministry. A pastor for over thirty years, Chip is the author of many books, including *Marriage That Works*, *Culture Shock*, *The Real Heaven*, *The Real God*, *The Invisible War*, and *Love, Sex, and Lasting Relationships*. Chip and his wife, Theresa, have four grown children and twelve grandchildren and live in California.

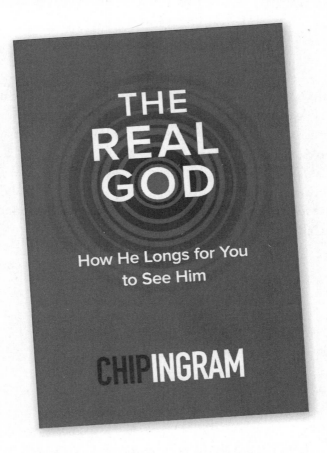

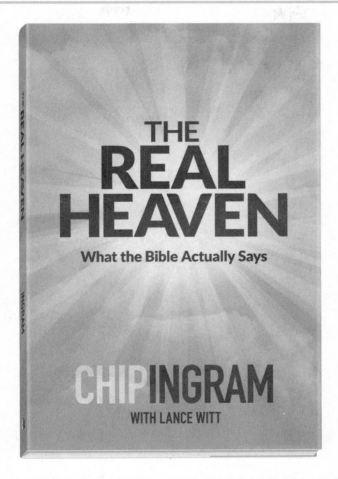

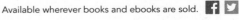

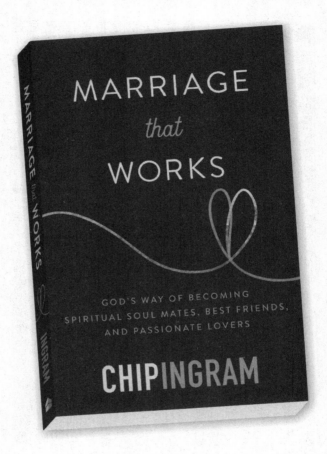

Also Available from
CHIP INGRAM

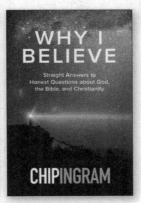

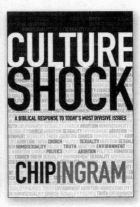

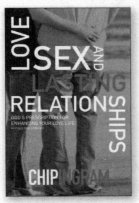

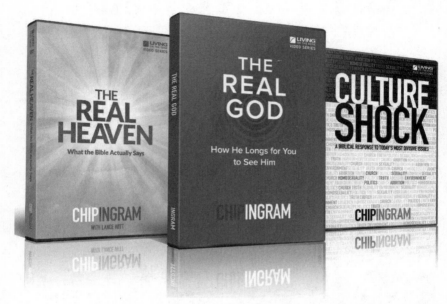